The Constitution of
The State of Nevada:
A Quick Reference Guide

Bootblack Budget Books
Copyright 2018 ©
ISBN-13: 978-1987710762
ISBN-10: 1987710762

**Contents:**

**Preliminary Action** – Page 28

**Ordinance** – Page 29

**Preamble** – Page 31

### Article I: Declaration of Rights – Page 32

**Section 1.** Inalienable Rights

**Section 2.** Purpose of Government; Paramount Allegiance to United States

**Section 3.** Trial by Jury; Waiver in Civil Cases

**Section 4.** Liberty of Conscience

**Section 5.** Suspension of Habeas Corpus

**Section 6.** Excessive Bail and Fines; Cruel or Unusual Punishments; Detention of Witnesses

**Section 7.** Bail; Exception for Capital Offenses and Certain Murders

**Section 8.** Rights of Accused in Criminal Prosecutions; Jeopardy; Rights of Victims of Crime; Due Process of Law; Eminent Domain.

**Section 8a.** Rights of Victim of Crime

**Section 9.** Liberty of Speech and the Press

**Section 10.** Right to Assemble and to Petition

**Section 11.** Right to Keep and Bear Arms; Civil Power Supreme

**Section 12.** Quartering Soldier in Private House

**Section 13.** Representation Apportioned According to Population

**Section 14.** Exemption of Property From Execution; Imprisonment for Debt

**Section 15.** Bill of Attainder; Ex Post Facto Law; Obligation of Contract

**Section 16.** Rights of Foreigners / Repealed

**Section 17.** Slavery and Involuntary Servitude Prohibited

**Section 18.** Unreasonable Seizure and Search; Issuance of Warrants

**Section 19.** Treason

**Section 20.** Rights Retained by People

**Section 21.** Limitation on Recognition of Marriage

**Section 21.** Recognition of Marriage.

**Section 22.** Eminent Domain Proceedings: Restrictions and Requirements

**Section 23.** Open, Competitive Retail Electric Energy Market; Granting of Monopolies and Exclusive Franchises for Generation of Electricity Prohibited; Severability

## Article II: Right of Suffrage – Page 40

**Section 1.** Rights of Voters

**Section 2.** When Residence Not Gained or Lost

**Section 3.** Armed Forces Personnel / Repealed

**Section 4.** Privilege of Qualified Electors on General Election Day

**Section 5.** Voting by Ballot; Voting in Elections by Legislature

**Section 6.** Registration of Electors; Test of Electoral Qualifications

**Section 7.** Poll Tax: Levy and Purpose / Repealed

**Section 8.** Qualifications of Voters on Adoption or Rejection of Constitution

**Section 9.** Recall of Public Officers: Procedure and Limitations

**Section 10.** Limitation on Contributions to Campaign

## Article III: Distribution of Powers – Page 44

**Section 1.** Three Separate Departments; Separation of Powers; Legislative Review of Administrative Regulations

## Article IV: Legislative Department – Page 45

**Section 1.** Legislative Power Vested in Senate and Assembly

**Section 2.** Biennial Sessions of Legislature: Commencement; Limitation on Duration; Void Actions; Submission of Proposed Executive Budget

**Section 2a.** Special Sessions of Legislature: Procedure for Convening; Precedence; Limitations on Business and Duration; Void Actions

**Section 3.** Members of Assembly: Election and Term of Office; Eligibility for Office

**Section 4.** Senators: Election and Term of Office; Eligibility for Office

**Section 5.** Number of Senators and Members of Assembly; Apportionment

**Section 6.** Power of Houses to Judge Qualifications, Elections and Returns of Members; Selection of Officers; Rules of Proceedings; Punishment of Members

**Section 7.** Punishment of Nonmember

**Section 8.** Senators and Members of Assembly Ineligible for Certain Offices

**Section 9.** Federal Officers Ineligible for State Office; Exceptions

**Section 10.** Embezzler of Public Money Ineligible for Office; Disqualification for Bribery

**Section 11.** Privilege of Members: Freedom From Arrest on Civil Process

**Section 12.** Vacancy

**Section 13.** Quorum; Compelling Attendance

**Section 14.** Journal

**Section 15.** Open Sessions and Meetings; Adjournment for More Than 3 Days or to Another Place

**Section 16.** Bills May Originate in Either House; Amendment

**Section 17.** Act to Embrace One Subject Only; Title; Amendment

**Section 18.** Reading of Bill; Voting on Final Passage; Number of Members Necessary to Pass Bill or Joint Resolution; Signatures; Referral of Certain Measures to Voters; Consent Calendar

**Section 19.** Manner of Drawing Money From Treasury

**Section 20.** Certain Local and Special Laws Prohibited

**Section 21.** General Laws to Have Uniform Application

**Section 22.** Suit Against State

**Section 23.** Enacting Clause; Law to be Enacted by Bill

**Section 24.** Lotteries

**Section 25.** Uniform County and Township Government

**Section 26.** Boards of County Commissioners: Election and Duties

**Section 27.** Disqualification of Jurors; Elections

**Section 28.** Compensation of Legislative Officers and Employees; Increase or Decrease of Compensation

**Section 29.** Duration of Regular and Special Sessions / Repealed

**Section 30.** Homesteads: Exemption From Forced Sale; Joint Consent Required for Alienation; Recording of Declaration

**Section 31.** Property of Married Persons

**Section 32.** County Officers: Power of Legislature; Election, Duties and Compensation; Duties of County Clerks

**Section 33.** Compensation of Members of Legislature; Payment for Postage, Stationery and Other Expenses; Additional Allowances for Officers

**Section 34.** Election of United States Senators / Repealed

**Section 35.** Bills to be Presented to Governor; Approval; Disapproval and Reconsideration by Legislature; Failure of Governor to Return Bill

**Section 36.** Abolishment of County; Approval of Voters in County

**Section 37.** Continuity of Government in Case of Enemy Attack; Succession to Public Offices; Legislative Quorum Requirements; Relocation of Seat of Government

**Section 37a.** Consolidation of City and County Containing Seat of Government Into One Municipal Government; Separate Taxing Districts

**Section 38.** Use of Plant of Genus Cannabis for Medical Purposes

## Article V: Executive Department – Page 62

**Section 1.** Supreme Executive Power Vested in Governor

**Section 2.** Election and Term of Governor

**Section 3.** Eligibility; Qualifications; Number of Terms

**Section 4.** Returns of General Election Transmitted to Secretary of State; Canvass by Supreme Court; Declaration of Election

**Section 5.** Governor Is Commander in Chief of State Military Forces

**Section 6.** Transaction of Executive Business; Reports of Executive Officers

**Section 7.** Responsibility for Execution of Laws

**Section 8.** Vacancies Filled by Governor

**Section 9.** Special Sessions of Legislature: Authority of Governor; Limitations on Business and Duration; Void Actions

**Section 10.** Governor's Message

**Section 11.** Adjournment of Legislature by Governor

**Section 12.** Person Holding Federal Office Ineligible for Office of Governor

**Section 13.** Pardons, Reprieves and Commutations of Sentence; Remission of Fines and Forfeitures

**Section 14.** Remission of Fines and Forfeitures; Commutations and Pardons; Suspension of Sentence; Probation

**Section 14.** State Board of Pardons Commissioners; Remission of Fines and Forfeitures; Commutations and Pardons; Suspension of Sentence; Probation

**Section 15.** The Great Seal

**Section 16.** Grants and Commissions: Signatures and Seal

**Section 17.** Election, Term, Qualifications and Duties of Lieutenant Governor; President of Senate; President Pro-Tempore of Senate to Act as Governor in Certain Circumstances

**Section 18.** Vacancy in Office of Governor; Duties to Devolve Upon Lieutenant Governor

**Section 19.** Other State Officers: Election and Term of Office; Eligibility for Office

**Section 20.** Secretary of State: Duties

**Section 21.** Board of State Prison Commissioners; Board of Examiners; Examination of Claims

**Section 22.** Duties of Certain State Officers

## Article VI: Judicial Department – Page 71

**Section 1.** Judicial Power Vested in Court System

**Section 2.** Supreme Court: Composition; Staggered Terms of Justices; Holding of Court by Panels of Justices and Full Court

**Section 3.** Justices of Supreme Court: Election; Terms; Chief Justice

**Section 3a.** Court of Appeals: Composition; Panel of Judges; Appointment, Election and Terms of Judges; Chief Judge; Service of Judges as Supplemental District Judges

**Section 4.** Jurisdiction of Supreme Court and Court of Appeals; Appointment of Judge to Sit for Disabled or Disqualified Justice or Judge

**Section 5.** Judicial Districts; Election and Terms of District Judges

**Section 6.** District Courts: Jurisdiction; Referees; Family Court

**Section 7.** Terms of Courts

**Section 8.** Number, Qualifications, Terms of Office and Jurisdiction of Justices of the Peace; Appeals; Courts of Record

**Section 9.** Municipal Courts

**Section 10.** Fees or Perquisites of Judicial Officers

**Section 11.** Justices and Judges Ineligible for Other Offices

**Section 12.** Judge Not to Charge Jury Respecting Matters of Fact; Statement of Testimony and Declaration of Law

**Section 13.** Style of Process

**Section 14.** One Form of Civil Action

**Section 15.** Compensation of Justices and Judges

**Section 16.** Special Fee in Civil Action for Compensation of Judges

**Section 17.** Absence of Judicial Officer From State; Vacation of Office

**Section 18.** Territorial Judicial Officers Not Superseded Until Election and Qualification of Successors

**Section 19.** Administration of Court System by Chief Justice

**Section 20.** Filling of Vacancies Occurring Before Expiration of Term of Office in Supreme Court or Court of Appeals or Among District Judges; Commission on Judicial Selection

**Section 21.** Commission on Judicial Discipline; Code of Judicial Conduct

## Article VII: Impeachment and Removal From Office – Page 86

**Section 1.** Impeachment: Trial; Conviction

**Section 2.** Officers Subject to Impeachment

**Section 3.** Removal of Justices of Supreme Court, Judges of Court of Appeals and Judges of District Courts

**Section 4.** Removal of Other Civil Officers

## Article VIII: Municipal and Other Corporations – Page 88

**Section 1.** Corporations Formed Under General Laws; Municipal Corporations Formed Under Special Acts

**Section 2.** Corporate Property Subject to Taxation; Exemptions

**Section 3.** Individual Liability of Corporators

**Section 4.** Regulation of Corporations Incorporated Under Territorial Law

**Section 5.** Corporations May Sue and be Sued

**Section 6.** Circulation of Certain Bank Notes or Paper as Money Prohibited

**Section 7.** Eminent Domain by Corporations

**Section 8.** Municipal Corporations Formed Under General Laws

**Section 9.** Gifts or Loans of Public Money to Certain Corporations Prohibited

**Section 10.** Loans of Public Money to or Ownership of Stock in Certain Corporations by County or Municipal Corporation Prohibited

## Article IX: Finance and State Debt – Page 91

**Section 1.** Fiscal Year

**Section 2.** Annual Tax for State Expenses; Trust Funds for Industrial Accidents, Occupational Diseases and Public Employees' Retirement System; Administration of Public Employees' Retirement System

**Section 3.** State Indebtedness: Limitations and Exceptions

**Section 4.** Assumption of Debts of County, City or Corporation by State

**Section 5.** Proceeds From Fees for Licensing and Registration of Motor Vehicles and Excise Taxes on Fuel Reserved for Construction, Maintenance and Repair of Public Highways; Exception

## Article X: Taxation – Page 94

**Section 1.** Uniform and Equal Rate of Assessment and Taxation; Valuation of Property; Exceptions and Exemptions; Inheritance and Personal Income Taxes Prohibited

**Section 1.** Uniform and Equal Rate of Assessment and Taxation; Valuation of Property; Exceptions and Exemptions; Inheritance and Personal Income Taxes Prohibited; Program for Refunds of Property Taxes to Seniors and Persons with Disabilities

**Section 2.** Total Tax Levy for Public Purposes Limited

**Section 3.** Household Goods and Furniture of Single Household Exempt From Taxation

**Section 3a.** Food Exempt From Taxes on Retail Sales; Exceptions

**Section 3b.** Durable Medical Equipment, Oxygen Delivery Equipment and Mobility Enhancing Equipment Exempt From Taxes on Retail Sales

**Section 4.** Taxation of Estates Taxed by United States; Limitations

**Section 5.** Tax on Proceeds of Minerals; Appropriation to Counties; Apportionment; Assessment and Taxation of Mines

**Section 6.** Enactment of Exemption From Ad Valorem Tax on Property or Excise Tax on Retail Sales

## Article XI: Education – Page 103

**Section 1.** Legislature to Encourage Education; Appointment, Term and Duties of Superintendent of Public Instruction

**Section 2.** Uniform System of Common Schools

**Section 3.** Pledge of Certain Property and Money, Escheated Estates and Fines Collected Under Penal Laws for Educational Purposes; Apportionment and Use of Interest

**Section 4.** Establishment of State University; Legislature to Provide by Law for Governance, Control and Management of State University and Protection of Academic Freedom

**Section 5.** Establishment of Normal Schools and Grades of Schools; Oath of Teachers and Professors

**Section 6.** Support of University and Common Schools by Direct Legislative Appropriation; Priority of Appropriations

**Section 7.** Board of Regents: Election and Duties

**Section 8.** Immediate Organization and Maintenance of State University

**Section 9.** Sectarian Instruction Prohibited in Common Schools and University

**Section 10.** No Public Money to be Used for Sectarian Purposes

### Article XII: Militia – Page 108

**Section 1.** Legislature to Provide for Militia

**Section 2.** Power of Governor to Call Out Militia

## Article XIII: Public Institutions — Page 109

**Section 1.** Institutions for Insane, Blind, Deaf and Dumb to be Fostered and Supported by State

**Section 2.** State Prison: Establishment and Maintenance; Juvenile Offenders

**Section 3.** County Public Welfare. / Repealed

**Article XIV: Boundary** – Page 110

**Section 1.** Boundary of the State of Nevada

## Article XV: Miscellaneous Provisions – Page 111

**Section 1.** Carson City Seat of Government

**Section 2.** Oath of Office

**Section 3.** Eligibility for Public Office

**Section 4.** Perpetuities; Eleemosynary Purposes

**Section 5.** Time of General Election

**Section 6.** Number of Members of Legislature Limited

**Section 7.** County Offices At County Seats

**Section 8.** Publication of General Statutes; Publication and Effective Date of Decisions of Supreme Court and Court of Appeals

**Section 9.** Increase or Decrease of Compensation of Officers Whose Compensation Fixed by Constitution

**Section 10.** Election or Appointment of Officers

**Section 11.** Term of Office When Not Fixed by Constitution; Limitation; Municipal Officers and Employees

**Section 12.** Certain State Officers to Keep Offices At Carson City

**Section 13.** Census by Legislature and Congress: Basis of Representation in Houses of Legislature

**Section 14.** Election by Plurality

**Section 15.** Merit System Governing Employment in Executive Branch of State Government

**Section 16.** Payment of Minimum Compensation to Employees

**Section 17.** Emergency Medical Services: Hospital or Independent Facility for Emergency Medical Care Prohibited From Denying Treatment Regardless of Whether Person Has Health Insurance; Establishment of Reasonable Cost for Services; Legislature May Set Different Rate If Commission Established to Ensure Services Provided At Reasonable Cost

## Article XVI: Amendments – Page 119

**Section 1.** Constitutional Amendments: Procedure; Concurrent and Consecutive Amendments

**Section 2.** Convention for Revision of Constitution: Procedure

## Article XVII: Schedule – Page 121

**Section 1.** Saving Existing Rights and Liabilities

**Section 2.** Territorial Laws to Remain in Force

**Section 3.** Fines, Penalties and Forfeitures to Inure to State

**Section 4.** Existing Obligations and Pending Suits

**Section 5.** Salaries of State Officers for First Term of Office

**Section 6.** Apportionment of Senators and Members of Assembly

**Section 7.** Assumption of Territorial Debts and Liabilities

**Section 8.** Terms of Elected State Officers

**Section 9.** Terms of Senators

**Section 10.** Terms of Senators and Members of Assembly After 1866

**Section 11.** Terms of Members of Assembly Elected At First General Election or in 1865

**Section 12.** Commencement Date of First Three Legislative Sessions; Regular Sessions of Legislature to be Held Biennially

**Section 13.** Continuation of Territorial County and Township Officers; Probate Judges

**Section 14.** Duties of Certain Territorial Officers Continued

**Section 15.** Terms of Supreme Court and District Courts

**Section 16.** Salaries of District Judges

**Section 17.** Alteration of Salary of District Judge Authorized

**Section 18.** Qualification and Terms of Certain Elective State Officers

**Section 19.** When Justices of Supreme Court and District Judges Enter Upon Duties

**Section 20.** State Officers and District Judges to be Commissioned by Territorial Governor; State Controller and Treasurer to Furnish Bonds

**Section 21.** Support of County and City Officers

**Section 22.** Vacancies in Certain State Offices: How Filled

**Section 23.** Civil and Criminal Cases Pending in Probate Courts Transferred to District Courts

**Section 24.** Levy of Tax Limited for 3 Years

**Section 25.** Roop County Attached to Washoe County

**Section 26.** Constitutional Debates and Proceedings: Publication; Payment of Reporter

## Article XVIII: Right of Suffrage
## (Repealed) – Page 131

**Section 1.** Rights of Suffrage and Officeholding / Repealed

## Article XIX: Initiative and Referendum – Page 132

**Section 1.** Referendum for Approval or Disapproval of Statute or Resolution Enacted by Legislature

**Section 2.** Initiative Petition for Enactment or Amendment of Statute or Amendment of Constitution; Concurrent and Consecutive Amendments

**Section 3.** Referendum and Initiative Petitions: Contents and Form; Signatures; Enacting Clause; Manner of Verification of Signatures

**Section 4.** Powers of Initiative and Referendum of Registered Voters of Counties and Municipalities

**Section 5.** Provisions of Article Self-Executing; Legislative Procedures

**Section 6.** Limitation on Initiative Making Appropriation or Requiring Expenditure of Money

**Election Ordinance** – Page 139

**Ordinances** – Page 139

## PRELIMINARY ACTION

Whereas,

The Act of Congress Approved March Twenty First A.D. Eighteen Hundred and Sixty Four "to enable the People of the Territory of Nevada to form a Constitution and State Government and for the admission of such State into the Union on an equal footing with the Original States," requires that the Members of the Convention for framing said Constitution shall, after Organization, on behalf of the people of said Territory, adopt the Constitution of the United States. — Therefore, be it Resolved,

That the Members of this Convention, elected by the Authority of the aforesaid enabling Act of Congress, Assembled in Carson City the Capital of said Territory of Nevada, and immediately subsequent to its Organization, do adopt, on behalf of the people of said Territory the Constitution of the United States.

## ORDINANCE

**Slavery Prohibited; Freedom of Religious Worship; Disclaimer of Public Lands** (Effective until the date Congress consents to amendment or a legal determination is made that such consent is not necessary.)

In obedience to the requirements of an act of the Congress of the United States, approved March twenty-first, A.D. eighteen hundred and sixty-four, to enable the people of Nevada to form a constitution and state government, this convention, elected and convened in obedience to said enabling act, do ordain as follows, and this ordinance shall be irrevocable, without the consent of the United States and the people of the State of Nevada:

**First.** That there shall be in this state neither slavery nor involuntary servitude, otherwise than in the punishment for crimes, whereof the party shall have been duly convicted.

**Second.** That perfect toleration of religious sentiment shall be secured, and no inhabitant of said state shall ever be molested, in person or property, on account of his or her mode of religious worship.

**Third.** That the people inhabiting said territory do agree and declare, that they forever disclaim all right and title to the unappropriated public lands lying within said territory, and that the same shall be and remain at the sole and entire disposition of the United States; and that lands belonging to citizens of the United States, residing without the said state, shall never be taxed higher than the land belonging to the residents thereof; and that no taxes shall be imposed by said state on lands or property therein belonging to, or which may hereafter be purchased by, the United States, unless otherwise provided by the congress of the United States.

**Slavery Prohibited; Freedom of Religious Worship; Taxation of Certain Property** (Effective on the date Congress consents to amendment or a legal determination is made that such consent is not necessary.)

In obedience to the requirements of an act of the Congress of the United States, approved March twenty-first, A.D. eighteen hundred and sixty-four, to enable the people of Nevada to form a constitution and state government, this convention, elected and convened in obedience to said enabling act, do ordain as follows, and this ordinance shall be irrevocable, without the consent of the United States and the people of the State of Nevada:

**First.** That there shall be in this state neither slavery nor involuntary servitude, otherwise than in the punishment for crimes, whereof the party shall have been duly convicted.

Second. That perfect toleration of religious sentiment shall be secured, and no inhabitant of said state shall ever be molested, in person or property, on account of his or her mode of religious worship.

**Third.** That the people inhabiting said territory do agree and declare, that lands belonging to citizens of the United States, residing without the said state, shall never be taxed higher than the land belonging to the residents thereof; and that no taxes shall be imposed by said state on lands or property therein belonging to, or which may hereafter be purchased by, the United States, unless otherwise provided by the Congress of the United States.

## **PREAMBLE**

We the people of the State of Nevada Grateful to Almighty God for our freedom in order to secure its blessings, insure domestic tranquility, and form a more perfect Government, do establish this Constitution.

## Article I: Declaration of Rights:

### Section 1. Inalienable Rights

All men are by Nature free and equal and have certain inalienable rights among which are those of enjoying and defending life and liberty; Acquiring, Possessing and Protecting property and pursuing and obtaining safety and happiness.

### Section 2. Purpose of Government; Paramount Allegiance to United States

All political power is inherent in the people. Government is instituted for the protection, security and benefit of the people; and they have the right to alter or reform the same whenever the public good may require it. But the Paramount Allegiance of every citizen is due to the Federal Government in the exercise of all its Constitutional powers as the same have been or may be defined by the Supreme Court of the United States; and no power exists in the people of this or any other State of the Federal Union to dissolve their connection therewith or perform any act tending to impair, subvert, or resist the Supreme Authority of the government of the United States. The Constitution of the United States confers full power on the Federal Government to maintain and Perpetuate its existence [existence], and whensoever any portion of the States, or people thereof attempt to secede from the Federal Union, or forcibly resist the Execution of its laws, the Federal Government may, by warrant of the Constitution, employ armed force in compelling obedience to its Authority.

### Section 3. Trial by Jury; Waiver in Civil Cases

The right of trial by Jury shall be secured to all and remain inviolate forever; but a Jury trial may be waived by the parties in all civil cases in the manner to be prescribed by law; and in civil cases, if three fourths of the Jurors agree upon a verdict it shall stand and have the same force and effect as a verdict by the whole Jury, Provided, the Legislature by a law passed by a two thirds vote of all the members elected to each branch thereof may require a unanimous verdict notwithstanding this Provision.

## Section 4. Liberty of Conscience

The free exercise and enjoyment of religious profession and worship without discrimination or preference shall forever be allowed in this State, and no person shall be rendered incompetent to be a witness on account of his opinions on matters of his religious belief, but the liberty of consciene [conscience] hereby secured, shall not be so construed, as to excuse acts of licentiousness or justify practices inconsistent with the peace, or safety of this State.

## Section 5. Suspension of Habeas Corpus

The privilege of the writ of Habeas Corpus, shall not be suspended unless when in cases of rebellion or invasion the public safety may require its suspension.

## Section 6. Excessive Bail and Fines; Cruel or Unusual Punishments; Detention of Witnesses

Excessive bail shall not be required, nor excessive fines imposed, nor shall cruel or unusual punishments be inflicted, nor shall witnesses be unreasonably detained.

## Section 7. Bail; Exception for Capital Offenses and Certain Murders

All persons shall be bailable by sufficient sureties; unless for Capital Offenses or murders punishable by life imprisonment without possibility of parole when the proof is evident or the presumption great.

## Section 8. Rights of Accused in Criminal Prosecutions; Jeopardy; Rights of Victims of Crime; Due Process of Law; Eminent Domain

**1.** No person shall be tried for a capital or other infamous crime (except in cases of impeachment, and in cases of the militia when in actual service and the land and naval forces in time of war, or which this State may keep, with the consent of Congress, in time of peace, and in cases of petit larceny, under the regulation of the Legislature) except on presentment or indictment of the grand jury, or upon information duly filed by a district attorney, or Attorney General of the State, and in any trial, in any court whatever, the party accused shall be allowed to appear and defend in person, and with counsel, as in civil actions. No person shall be subject to be twice put in jeopardy for the same offense; nor shall he be compelled, in any criminal case, to be a witness against himself.

**2.** The Legislature shall provide by law for the rights of victims of crime, personally or through a representative, to be:

**(a)** Informed, upon written request, of the status or disposition of a criminal proceeding at any stage of the proceeding;

**(b)** Present at all public hearings involving the critical stages of a criminal proceeding; and

**(c)** Heard at all proceedings for the sentencing or release of a convicted person after trial.

**3.** Except as otherwise provided in subsection 4, no person may maintain an action against the State or any public officer or employee for damages or injunctive, declaratory or other legal or equitable relief on behalf of a victim of a crime as a result of a violation of any statute enacted by the Legislature pursuant to subsection 2. No such violation authorizes setting aside a conviction or sentence or continuing or postponing a criminal proceeding.

**4.** A person may maintain an action to compel a public officer or employee to carry out any duty required by the Legislature pursuant to subsection 2.

**5.** No person shall be deprived of life, liberty, or property, without due process of law.

**6.** Private property shall not be taken for public use without just compensation having been first made, or secured, except in cases of war, riot, fire, or great public peril, in which case compensation shall be afterward made.

## Section 9. Liberty of Speech and the Press

Every citizen may freely speak, write and publish his sentiments on all subjects being responsible for the abuse of that right; and no law shall be passed to restrain or abridge the liberty of speech or of the press. in all criminal prosecutions and civil actions for libels, the truth may be given in evidence to the Jury; and if it shall appear to the Jury that the matter charged as libelous is true and was published with good motives and for justifiable ends, the party shall be acquitted or exonerated.

## Section 10. Right to Assemble and to Petition

The people shall have the right freely to assemble together to consult for the common good, to instruct their representatives and to petition the Legislature for redress of Grievances.

## Section 11. Right to Keep and Bear Arms; Civil Power Supreme

**1.** Every citizen has the right to keep and bear arms for security and defense, for lawful hunting and recreational use and for other lawful purposes.

**2.** The military shall be subordinate to the civil power; No standing army shall be maintained by this State in time of peace, and in time of War, no appropriation for a standing army shall be for a longer time than two years.

### Section 12. Quartering Soldier in Private House

No soldier shall, in time of Peace be quartered in any house without the consent of the owner, nor in time of War, except in the manner to be prescribed by law.

### Section 13. Representation Apportioned According to Population

Representation shall be apportioned according to population.

### Section 14. Exemption of Property from Execution; Imprisonment for Debt

The privilege of the debtor to enjoy the necessary comforts of life shall be recognized by wholesome laws, exempting a reasonable amount of property from seizure or sale for payment of any debts or liabilities hereafter contracted; and there shall be no imprisonment for debt, except in cases of fraud, libel, or slander, and no person shall be imprisioned [imprisoned] for a Militia fine in time of Peace.

### Section 15. Bill of Attainder; Ex Post Facto Law; Obligation of Contract

No bill of attainder, ex-post-facto law, or law impairing the obligation of contracts shall ever be passed.

### Section 16. Rights of Foreigners

Repealed.

## Section 17. Slavery and Involuntary Servitude Prohibited

Neither Slavery nor involuntary servitude unless for the punishment of crimes shall ever be tolerated in this State.

## Section 18. Unreasonable Seizure and Search; Issuance of Warrants

The right of the people to be secure in their persons, houses, papers and effects against unreasonable seizures and searches shall not be violated; and no warrant shall issue but on probable cause, supported by Oath or Affirmation, particularly describing the place or places to be searched, and the person or persons, and thing or things to be seized.

## Section 19. Treason

Treason against the State shall consist only in levying war against it, adhering to its enemies or giving them Aid and Comfort. and no person shall be convicted of treason unless on the testimony of two witnesses to the same overt act, or on confession in open court.

## Section 20. Rights Retained by People

This enumeration of rights shall not be construed to impair or deny others retained by the people.

## Section 21. Limitation on Recognition of Marriage

Only a marriage between a male and female person shall be recognized and given effect in this state.
Amendments

## Section 22. Eminent Domain Proceedings: Restrictions and Requirements

Notwithstanding any other provision of this Constitution to the contrary:

**1.** Public use shall not include the direct or indirect transfer of any interest in property taken in an eminent domain proceeding from one private party to another private party. in all eminent domain actions, the government shall have the burden to prove public use.

**2.** in all eminent domain actions, prior to the government's occupancy, a property owner shall be given copies of all appraisals by the government and shall be entitled, at the property owner's election, to a separate and distinct determination by a district court jury, as to whether the taking is actually for a public use.

**3.** If a public use is determined, the taken or damaged property shall be valued at its highest and best use without considering any future dedication requirements imposed by the government. If private property is taken for any proprietary governmental purpose, then the property shall be valued at the use to which the government intends to put the property, if such use results in a higher value for the land taken.

**4.** in all eminent domain actions, just compensation shall be defined as that sum of money, necessary to place the property owner back in the same position, monetarily, without any governmental offsets, as if the property had never been taken. Just compensation shall include, but is not limited to, compounded interest and all reasonable costs and expenses actually incurred.

**5.** in all eminent domain actions where fair market value is applied, it shall be defined as the highest price the property would bring on the open market.

**6.** Property taken in eminent domain shall automatically revert back to the original property owner upon repayment of the original purchase price, if the property is not used within five years for the original purpose stated by the government. The five years shall begin running from the date of the entry of the final order of condemnation.

**7.** A property owner shall not be liable to the government for attorney fees or costs in any eminent domain action.

8. for all provisions contained in this section, government shall be defined as the State of Nevada, its political subdivisions, agencies, any public or private agent acting on their behalf, and any public or private entity that has the power of eminent domain.

**9.** Any provision contained in this section shall be deemed a separate and freestanding right and shall remain in full force and effect should any other provision contained in this section be stricken for any reason.

## Article II: Right of Suffrage

### Section 1. Right to Vote; Qualifications of Elector; Qualifications of Nonelector to Vote for President and Vice President of United States

All citizens of the United States (not laboring under the disabilities named in this constitution) of the age of eighteen years and upwards, who shall have actually, and not constructively, resided in the state six months, and in the district or county thirty days next preceding any election, shall be entitled to vote for all officers that now or hereafter may be elected by the people, and upon all questions submitted to the electors at such election; provided, that no person who has been or may be convicted of treason or felony in any state or territory of the United States, unless restored to civil rights, and no person who has been adjudicated mentally incompetent, unless restored to legal capacity, shall be entitled to the privilege of an elector. There shall be no denial of the elective franchise at any election on account of sex. The legislature may provide by law the conditions under which a citizen of the United States who does not have the status of an elector in another state and who does not meet the residence requirements of this section may vote in this state for President and Vice President of the United States.

### Section 2. When Residence Not Gained or Lost

for the purpose of voting, no person shall be deemed to have gained or lost a residence solely by reason of his presence or absence while employed in the service of the United States, nor while engaged in the navigation of the waters of the United States or of the high seas; nor while a student of any institution of learning; nor while kept at any charitable institution or medical facility at public expense; nor while confined in any public prison.

## Section 3. Armed Forces Personnel

Repealed.

## Section 4. Privilege of Qualified Electors on General Election Day

During the day on which any General Election shall be held in this State no qualified elector shall be arrested by virtue of any civil process.

## Section 5. Voting by Ballot; Voting in Elections by Legislature

All elections by the people shall be by ballot, and all elections by the Legislature, or by either branch thereof shall be "Viva-Voce".

## Section 6. Registration of Electors; Test of Electoral Qualifications

Provision shall be made by law for the registration of the names of the Electors within the counties of which they may be residents and for the ascertainment by proper proofs of the persons who shall be entitled to the right of suffrage, as hereby established, to preserve the purity of elections, and to regulate the manner of holding and making returns of the same; and the Legislature shall have power to prescribe by law any other or further rules or oaths, as may be deemed necessary, as a test of electoral qualification.

## Section 7. Poll Tax: Levy and Purpose

Repealed.

## Section 8. Qualifications of Voters on Adoption or Rejection of Constitution

All persons qualified by law to vote for representatives to the General Assembly of the Territory of Nevada, on the twenty first day of March A.D. Eighteen hundred and sixty four and all other persons who may be lawful voters in said Territory on the first Wednesday of September next following, shall be entitled to vote directly upon the question of adopting or rejecting this Constitution.

## Section 9. Recall of Public Officers: Procedure and Limitations

Every public officer in the State of Nevada is subject, as herein provided, to recall from office by the registered voters of the state, or of the county, district, or municipality which he represents. for this purpose, not less than twenty-five percent (25%) of the number who actually voted in the state or in the county, district, or municipality which he represents, at the election in which he was elected, shall file their petition, in the manner herein provided, demanding his recall by the people. They shall set forth in said petition, in not exceeding two hundred (200) words, the reasons why said recall is demanded. If he shall offer his resignation, it shall be accepted and take effect on the day it is offered, and the vacancy thereby caused shall be filled in the manner provided by law. If he shall not resign within five (5) days after the petition is filed, a special election shall be ordered to be held within thirty (30) days after the issuance of the call therefore, in the state, or county, district, or municipality electing said officer, to determine whether the people will recall said officer. on the ballot at said election shall be printed verbatim as set forth in the recall petition, the reasons for demanding the recall of said officer, and in not more than two hundred (200) words, the officer's justification of his course in office. He shall continue to perform the duties of his office until the result of said election shall be finally declared. Other candidates for the office may be nominated to be voted for at said special election. The candidate who shall receive highest number of votes at said special election shall be deemed elected for the remainder of the term, whether it be the person against whom the recall petition was filed, or another. The recall petition shall be filed with the officer with whom the petition for nomination to such office shall be filed, and the same officer shall order the special election when it is required. No such petition shall be circulated or filed against any officer until he has actually held his office six (6) months, save and except that it may be filed against a senator or assemblyman in the legislature at any time after ten (10) days from the beginning of the first session after his election. After one such petition and special election, no further recall petition shall be filed against the same officer during the term for which he was elected, unless such further petitioners shall pay into the public treasury from which the expenses of said special election have been paid, the whole amount paid out of said public treasury as expenses for the preceding special election. Such additional legislation as may aid the operation of this section shall be provided by law.

### Section 10. Limitation on Contributions to Campaign

**1.** as used in this Section, "contribution" includes the value of services provided in kind for which money would otherwise be paid, such as paid polling and resulting data, paid direct mail, paid solicitation by telephone, any paid campaign paraphernalia printed or otherwise produced, and the use of paid personnel to assist in a campaign.

**2.** The Legislature shall provide by law for the limitation of the total contribution by any natural or artificial person to the campaign of any person for election to any office, except a federal office, to $5,000 for the primary and $5,000 for the general election, and to the approval or rejection of any question by the registered voters to $5,000, whether the office sought or the question submitted is local or for the State as a whole. The Legislature shall further provide for the punishment of the contributor, the candidate, and any other knowing party to a violation of the limit, as a felony.

## Article III: Distribution of Powers

### Section 1. Three Separate Departments; Separation of Powers; Legislative Review of Administrative Regulations

**1.** The powers of the Government of the State of Nevada shall be divided into three separate departments,—the Legislative,— the Executive and the Judicial; and no persons charged with the exercise of powers properly belonging to one of these departments shall exercise any functions, appertaining to either of the others, except in the cases expressly directed or permitted in this constitution.

**2.** If the legislature authorizes the adoption of regulations by an executive agency which bind persons outside the agency, the legislature may provide by law for:

**(a)** The review of these regulations by a legislative agency before their effective date to determine initially whether each is within the statutory authority for its adoption;

**(b)** The suspension by a legislative agency of any such regulation which appears to exceed that authority, until it is reviewed by a legislative body composed of members of the Senate and Assembly which is authorized to act on behalf of both houses of the legislature; and

**(c)** The nullification of any such regulation by a majority vote of that legislative body, whether or not the regulation was suspended.

## Article IV: Legislative Department

### Section 1. Legislative Power Vested in Senate and Assembly

The Legislative authority of this State shall be vested in a Senate and Assembly which shall be designated "The Legislature of the State of Nevada" and the sessions of such Legislature shall be held at the seat of government of the State.

### Section 2. Biennial Sessions of Legislature: Commencement; Limitation on Duration; Void Actions; Submission of Proposed Executive Budget

**1.** The sessions of the Legislature shall be biennial, and shall commence on the 1st Monday of February following the election of members of the Assembly, unless the Governor of the State or the members of the Legislature shall, in the interim, convene the Legislature by proclamation or petition.

**2.** The Legislature shall adjourn sine die each regular session not later than midnight Pacific time at the end of the 120th consecutive calendar day of that session, inclusive of the day on which that session commences. Any legislative action taken after midnight Pacific time at the end of the 120th consecutive calendar day of that session is void, unless the legislative action is conducted during a special session. 3. The Governor shall submit the proposed executive budget to the Legislature not later than 14 calendar days before the commencement of each regular session.

**4.** for the purposes of this section, "midnight Pacific time" must be determined based on the actual measure of time that, on the final calendar day of the session, is being used and observed by the general population as the uniform time for the portion of Nevada which lies within the Pacific time zone, or any legal successor to the Pacific time zone, and which includes the seat of government of this State as designated by Section 1 of Article 15 of this Constitution. The Legislature and its members, officers and employees shall not employ any device, pretense or fiction that adjusts, evades or ignores this measure of time for the purpose of extending the duration of the session.

## Section 2a. Special Sessions of Legislature: Procedure for Convening; Precedence; Limitations on Business and Duration; Void Actions

**1.** The Legislature may be convened, on extraordinary occasions, upon a petition signed by two-thirds of the members elected to each House of the Legislature. A petition must specify the business to be transacted during the special session, indicate a date on or before which the Legislature is to convene and be transmitted to the Secretary of State. Upon receipt of one or more substantially similar petitions signed, in the aggregate, by the required number of members, calling for a special session, the Secretary of State shall notify all members of the Legislature and the Governor that a special session will be convened pursuant to this section.

**2.** At a special session convened pursuant to this section, the Legislature shall not introduce, consider or pass any bills except those related to the business specified in the petition and those necessary to provide for the expenses of the session.

**3.** A special session convened pursuant to this section takes precedence over a special session convened by the Governor pursuant to Section 9 of Article 5 of this Constitution, unless otherwise provided in the petition convening the special session pursuant to this section.

**4.** The Legislature may provide by law for the procedure for convening a special session pursuant to this section.

**5.** Except as otherwise provided in this subsection, the Legislature shall adjourn sine die a special session convened pursuant to this section not later than midnight Pacific time at the end of the 20th consecutive calendar day of that session, inclusive of the day on which that session commences. Any legislative action taken after midnight Pacific time at the end of the 20th consecutive calendar day of that session is void. This subsection does not apply to a special session that is convened to conduct proceedings for:

**(a)** Impeachment or removal from office of the Governor and other state and judicial officers pursuant to Article 7 of this Constitution; or

**(b)** Expulsion from office of a member of the Legislature pursuant to Section 6 of Article 4 of this Constitution.

**6.** for the purposes of this section, "midnight Pacific time" must be determined based on the actual measure of time that, on the final calendar day of the session, is being used and observed by the general population as the uniform time for the portion of Nevada which lies within the Pacific time zone, or any legal successor to the Pacific time zone, and which includes the seat of government of this State as designated by Section 1 of Article 15 of this Constitution. The Legislature and its members, officers and employees shall not employ any device, pretense or fiction that adjusts, evades or ignores this measure of time for the purpose of extending the duration of the session.

### Section 3. Members of Assembly: Election and Term of Office; Eligibility for Office

**1.** The members of the Assembly shall be chosen biennially by the qualified electors of their respective districts, on the Tuesday next after the first Monday in November and their term of Office shall be two years from the day next after their election.

**2.** No person may be elected or appointed as a member of the Assembly who has served in that Office, or at the expiration of his current term if he is so serving will have served, 12 years or more, from any district of this State.

## Section 4.  Senators: Election and Term of Office; Eligibility for Office

**1.** Senators shall be chosen at the same time and places as members of the Assembly by the qualified electors of their respective districts, and their term of Office shall be four years from the day next after their election.

**2.** No person may be elected or appointed as a Senator who has served in that Office, or at the expiration of his current term if he is so serving will have served, 12 years or more, from any district of this State.

## Section 5.  Number of Senators and Assemblymen; Apportionment

Senators and members of the Assembly shall be duly qualified electors in the respective counties and districts which they represent, and the number of Senators shall not be less than one-third nor more than one-half of that of the members of the Assembly.

It shall be the mandatory duty of the Legislature at its first session after the taking of the decennial census of the United States in the year 1950, and after each subsequent decennial census, to fix by law the number of Senators and Assemblymen, and apportion them among the several counties of the State, or among legislative districts which may be established by law, according to the number of inhabitants in them, respectively.

## Section 6.  Power of Houses to Judge Qualifications, Elections and Returns of Members; Selection of Officers; Rules of Proceedings; Punishment of Members

Each House shall judge of the qualifications, elections and returns of its own members, choose its own officers (except the President of the Senate), determine the rules of its proceedings and may punish its members for disorderly conduct, and with the concurrence of two thirds of all the members elected, expel a member.

## Section 7. Punishment of Nonmember

Either House, during the session, may punish, by imprisonment, any person not a member, who shall have been guilty of disrespect to the House by disorderly or contemptuous behavior in its presence; but such imprisonment shall not extend beyond the final adjournment of the session.

## Section 8. Senators and Assemblymen Ineligible for Certain Offices

No Senator or member of Assembly shall, during the term for which he shall have been elected, nor for one year thereafter be appointed to any civil office of profit under this State which shall have been created, or the emoluments of which shall have been increased during such term, except such office as may be filled by elections by the people.

## Section 9. Federal Officers Ineligible for State Office; Exceptions

No person holding any lucrative office under the Government of the United States or any other power, shall be eligible to any civil office of Profit under this State; Provided, that Post-Masters whose compensation does not exceed Five Hundred dollars per annum, or commissioners of deeds, shall not be deemed as holding a lucrative office.

## Section 10. Embezzler of Public Money Ineligible for Office; Disqualification for Bribery

Any person who shall be convicted of the embezzlement, or defalcation of the public funds of this State or who may be convicted of having given or offered a bribe to procure his election or appointment to office, or received a bribe to aid in the procurement of office for any other person, shall be disqualified from holding any office of profit or trust in this State; and the Legislature shall, as soon as practicable, provide by law for the punishment of such defalcation, bribery, or embezzlement as a felony.

### Section 11. Privilege of Members: Freedom from Arrest on Civil Process

Members of the Legislature shall be privileged from arrest on civil process during the session of the Legislature, and for fifteen days next before the commencement of each session.

### Section 12. Vacancy

in case of the death or resignation of any member of the legislature, either senator or assemblyman, the county commissioners of the county from which such member was elected shall appoint a person of the same political party as the party which elected such senator or assemblyman to fill such vacancy; provided, that this section shall apply only in cases where no biennial election or any regular election at which county officers are to [be] elected takes place between the time of such death or resignation and the next succeeding session of the legislature.

### Section 13. Quorum; Compelling Attendance

A majority of all the members elected to each House shall constitute a quorum to transact business, but a smaller number may adjourn, from day to day and may compel the attendance of absent members, in such manner, and under such penalties as each house may prescribe.

## Section 14. Journal

Each House shall keep a journal of its own proceedings which shall be published and the yeas and nays of the members of either house on any question shall at the desire of any three members present, be entered on the journal.

## Section 15. Open Sessions and Meetings; Adjournment for More Than 3 Days or to Another Place

The doors of each House shall be kept open during its session, and neither shall, without the consent of the other, adjourn for more than three days nor to any other place than that in which they may be holding their sessions. The meetings of all legislative committees must be open to the public, except meetings held to consider the character, alleged misconduct, professional competence, or physical or mental health of a person.

## Section 16. Bills May Originate in Either House; Amendment

Any bill may originate in either House of the Legislature, and all bills passed by one may be amended in the other.

## Section 17. Act to Embrace One Subject Only; Title; Amendment

Each law enacted by the Legislature shall embrace but one subject, and matter, properly connected therewith, which subject shall be briefly expressed in the title; and no law shall be revised or amended by reference to its title only; but, in such case, the act as revised or section as amended, shall be re-enacted and published at length.

## Section 18. Reading of Bill; Voting on Final Passage; Number of Members Necessary to Pass Bill or Joint Resolution; Signatures; Referral of Certain Measures to Voters; Consent Calendar

**1.** Every bill, except a bill placed on a consent calendar adopted as provided in subsection 4, must be read by sections on three several days, in each House, unless in case of emergency, two thirds of the House where such bill is pending shall deem it expedient to dispense with this rule. The reading of a bill by sections, on its final passage, shall in no case be dispensed with, and the vote on the final passage of every bill or joint resolution shall be taken by yeas and nays to be entered on the journals of each House. Except as otherwise provided in subsection 2, a majority of all the members elected to each House is necessary to pass every bill or joint resolution, and all bills or joint resolutions so passed, shall be signed by the presiding officers of the respective Houses and by the Secretary of the Senate and Clerk of the Assembly.

**2.** Except as otherwise provided in subsection 3, an affirmative vote of not fewer than two-thirds of the members elected to each House is necessary to pass a bill or joint resolution which creates, generates, or increases any public revenue in any form, including but not limited to taxes, fees, assessments and rates, or changes in the computation bases for taxes, fees, assessments and rates.

**3.** A majority of all of the members elected to each House may refer any measure which creates, generates, or increases any revenue in any form to the people of the State at the next general election, and shall become effective and enforced only if it has been approved by a majority of the votes cast on the measure at such election.

**4.** Each House may provide by rule for the creation of a consent calendar and establish the procedure for the passage of uncontested bills.

## Section 19. Manner of Drawing Money from Treasury

No money shall be drawn from the treasury but in consequence of appropriations made by law.

## Section 20. Certain Local and Special Laws Prohibited

The legislature shall not pass local or special laws in any of the following enumerated cases—that is to say:

Regulating the jurisdiction and duties of justices of the peace and of constables, and fixing their compensation;

for the punishment of crimes and misdemeanors;

Regulating the practice of courts of justice;

Providing for changing the venue in civil and criminal cases; Granting divorces;

Changing the names of persons;

Vacating roads, town plots, streets, alleys, and public squares;

Summoning and impaneling grand and petit juries, and providing for their compensation;

Regulating county and township business;

Regulating the election of county and township officers;

for the assessment and collection of taxes for state, county, and township purposes;

Providing for opening and conducting elections of state, county, or township officers, and designating the places of voting;

Providing for the sale of real estate belonging to minors or other persons laboring under legal disabilities;

Giving effect to invalid deeds, wills, or other instruments;

Refunding money paid into the state treasury, or into the treasury of any county;

Releasing the indebtedness, liability, or obligation of any corporation, association, or person to the state, or to any county, town, or city of this state; but nothing in this section shall be construed to deny or restrict the power of the legislature to establish and regulate the compensation and fees of county officers, to authorize and empower the boards of county commissioners of the various counties of the state to establish and regulate the compensation and fees of township officers in their respective counties, to establish and regulate the rates of freight, passage, toll, and charges of railroads, tollroads, ditch, flume, and tunnel companies incorporated under the laws of this state or doing business therein.

### Section 21. General Laws to Have Uniform Application

in all cases enumerated in the preceding section, and in all other cases where a general law can be made applicable, all laws shall be general and of uniform operation throughout the State.

### Section 22. Suit Against State

Provision may be made by general law for bringing suit against the State as to all liabilities originating after the adoption of this Constitution.

### Section 23. Enacting Clause; Law to be Enacted by Bill

The enacting clause of every law shall be as follows: "The people of the State of Nevada represented in Senate and Assembly, do enact as follows," and no law shall be enacted except by bill.

## Section 24. Lotteries

**1.** Except as otherwise provided in subsection 2, no lottery may be authorized by this State, nor may lottery tickets be sold.

**2.** The State and the political subdivisions thereof shall not operate a lottery. The Legislature may authorize persons engaged in charitable activities or activities not for profit to operate a lottery in the form of a raffle or drawing on their own behalf. All proceeds of the lottery, less expenses directly related to the operation of the lottery, must be used only to benefit charitable or nonprofit activities in this State. A charitable or nonprofit organization shall not employ or otherwise engage any person to organize or operate its lottery for compensation. The Legislature may provide by law for the regulation of such lotteries.

## Section 25. Uniform County and Township Government

The Legislature shall establish a system of County and Township Government which shall be uniform throughout the State.

## Section 26. Boards of County Commissioners: Election and Duties

The Legislature shall provide by law, for the election of a Board of County Commissioners in each County, and such County Commissioners shall jointly and individually perform such duties as may be prescribed by law.

## Section 27. Disqualification of Jurors; Elections

Laws shall be made to exclude from serving on juries, all persons not qualified electors of this State, and all persons who shall have been convicted of bribery, perjury, foregery [forgery,] larceny or other high crimes, unless restored to civil rights; and laws shall be passed regulating elections, and prohibiting under adequate penalties, all undue influence thereon from power, bribery, tumult, or other improper practice.

## Section 28. Compensation of Legislative Officers and Employees; Increase or Decrease of Compensation

No money shall be drawn from the State Treasury as salary or compensation to any officer or employee of the Legislature, or either branch thereof, except in cases where such salary or compensation has been fixed by a law in force prior to the election or appointment of such officer or employee; and the salary or compensation so fixed, shall neither be increased nor diminished so as to apply to any officer or employee of the Legislature, or either branch thereof at such Session; Provided, that this restriction shall not apply to the first session of the Legislature.

## Section 29. Duration of Regular and Special Sessions

Repealed.

## Section 30. Homesteads: Exemption from Forced Sale; Joint Consent Required for Alienation; Recording of Declaration

A homestead as provided by law, shall be exempt from forced sale under any process of law, and shall not be alienated without the joint consent of husband and wife when that relation exists; but no property shall be exempt from sale for taxes or for the payment of obligations contracted for the purchase of said premises, or for the erection of improvements thereon; Provided, the provisions of this Section shall not apply to any process of law obtained by virtue of a lien given by the consent of both husband and wife, and laws shall be enacted providing for the recording of such homestead within the County in which the same shall be situated.

## Section 31. Property of Married Persons

All property, both real and personal, of a married person owned or claimed by such person before marriage, and that acquired afterward by gift, devise or descent, shall be the separate property of such person. The legislature shall more clearly define the rights of married persons in relation to their separate property and other property.

## Section 32. County Officers: Power of Legislature; Election,

Duties and Compensation; Duties of County Clerks
The Legislature shall have power to increase, diminish, consolidate or abolish the following county officers: County Clerks, County Recorders, Auditors, Sheriffs, District Attorneys and Public Administrators. The Legislature shall provide for their election by the people, and fix by law their duties and compensation. County Clerks shall be ex-officio Clerks of the Courts of Record and of the Boards of County Commissioners in and for their respective counties.

## Section 33. Compensation of Members of Legislature; Payment for Postage, Stationery and Other Expenses; Additional Allowances for Officers

The members of the Legislature shall receive for their services a compensation to be fixed by law and paid out of the public treasury, for not to exceed 60 days during any regular session of the Legislature and not to exceed 20 days during any special session; but no increase of such compensation shall take effect during the term for which the members of either house shall have been elected; Provided, that an appropriation may be made for the payment of such actual expenses as members of the Legislature may incur for postage, express charges, newspapers and stationery not exceeding the sum of Sixty dollars for any general or special session to each member; and Furthermore Provided, that the Speaker of the Assembly, and Lieutenant

Governor, as President of the Senate, shall each, during the time of their actual attendance as such presiding officers receive an additional allowance of two dollars per diem.

## Section 33. Compensation of Members of Legislature; Payment for Expenses of Members; Additional Allowances for Officers

The members of the Legislature shall receive for their services a compensation to be fixed by law and paid out of the public treasury at regular intervals determined by law, but no increase of such compensation shall take effect during the term for which the members of either House shall have been elected; Provided, that an appropriation may be made for the payment of such actual expenses as members of the Legislature may incur for any regular or special session to each member; and Furthermore Provided, that the Speaker of the Assembly and Lieutenant Governor, as President of the Senate, shall each, during the time of their actual attendance as such presiding officers, receive an additional allowance of two dollars per diem.

## Section 34. Election of United States Senators

Repealed.

## Section 35. Bills to be Presented to Governor; Approval; Disapproval and Reconsideration by Legislature; Failure of Governor to Return Bill

Every bill which may have passed the Legislature, shall, before it becomes a law be presented to the Governor. If he approve it, he shall sign it, but if not he shall return it with his objections, to the House in which it originated, which House shall cause such objections to be entered upon its journal, and proceed to reconsider it; If after such reconsideration it again pass both Houses by yeas and nays, by a vote of two thirds of the members elected to each House it shall become a law notwithstanding the Governors objections. If any bill shall not be returned within five days after it shall have been presented to him (Sunday excepted) exclusive of the day on which he received it, the same shall be a law, in like manner as if he had signed it, unless the Legislature by its final adjournment, prevent such return, in which case it shall be a law, unless the Governor within ten days next after the adjournment (Sundays excepted) shall file such bill with his objections thereto, in the office of the Secretary of State, who shall lay the same before the Legislature at its next Session, in like manner as if it had been returned by the Governor, and if the same shall receive the vote of two-thirds of the members elected to each branch of the Legislature, upon a vote taken by yeas and nays to be entered upon the journals of each house, it shall become a law.

## Section 36. Abolishment of County; Approval of Voters in County

The legislature shall not abolish any county unless the qualified voters of the county affected shall at a general or special election first approve such proposed abolishment by a majority of all the voters voting at such election. The legislature shall provide by law the method of initiating and conducting such election.

## Section 37. Continuity of Government in Case of Enemy Attack; Succession to Public Offices; Legislative Quorum Requirements; Relocation of Seat of Government

The legislature, in order to insure continuity of state and local governmental operations in periods of emergency resulting from disasters caused by enemy attack, shall have the power and the immediate duty to provide for immediate and temporary succession to the powers and duties of public offices, of whatever nature and whether filled by election or appointment, the incumbents of which may become unavailable for carrying on the powers and duties of such offices, and to adopt such other measures as may be necessary and proper for insuring the continuity of governmental operations, including changes in quorum requirements in the legislature and the relocation of the seat of government. in the exercise of the powers hereby conferred, the legislature shall conform to the requirements of this constitution except to the extent that in the judgment of the legislature so to do would be impracticable or would admit of undue delay.

## Section 37A. Consolidation of City and County Containing Seat of Government into One Municipal Government; Separate Taxing Districts

Notwithstanding the general provisions of sections 20, 25, 26, and 36 of this article, the legislature may by law consolidate into one municipal government, with one set of officers, the city designated as the seat of government of this state and the county in which such city is situated. Such consolidated municipality shall be considered as a county for the purpose of representation in the legislature, shall have all the powers conferred upon counties by this constitution or by general law, and shall have such other powers as may be conferred by its charter. Notwithstanding the general provisions of section 1 of article 10, the legislature may create two or more separate taxing districts within such consolidated municipality.

## Section 38. Use of Plant of Genus Cannabis for Medical Purposes

**1.** The legislature shall provide by law for:

**(a)** The use by a patient, upon the advice of his physician, of a plant of the genus Cannabis for the treatment or alleviation of cancer, glaucoma, acquired immunodeficiency syndrome; severe, persistent nausea of cachexia resulting from these or other chronic or debilitating medical conditions; epilepsy and other disorders characterized by seizure; multiple sclerosis and other disorders characterized by muscular spasticity; or other conditions approved pursuant to law for such treatment.

**(b)** Restriction of the medical use of the plant by a minor to require diagnosis and written authorization by a physician, parental consent, and parental control of the acquisition and use of the plant.

**(c)** Protection of the plant and property related to its use from forfeiture except upon conviction or plea of guilty or nolo contendere for possession or use not authorized by or pursuant to this section.

**(d)** A registry of patients, and their attendants, who are authorized to use the plant for a medical purpose, to which law enforcement officers may resort to verify a claim of authorization and which is otherwise confidential.

**(e)** Authorization of appropriate methods for supply of the plant to patients authorized to use it.

**2. This section does not:**

**(a)** Authorize the use or possession of the plant for a purpose other than medical or use for a medical purpose in public.

**(b)** Require reimbursement by an insurer for medical use of the plant or accommodation of medical use in a place of employment.

## Article V - Executive Department

### Section 1. Supreme Executive Power Vested in Governor

The supreme executive power of this State, shall be vested in a Chief Magistrate who shall be Governor of the State of Nevada.

### Section 2. Election and Term of Governor

The Governor shall be elected by the qualified electors at the time and places of voting for members of the Legislature, and shall hold his office for Four Years from the time of his installation, and until his successor shall be qualified.

### Section 3. Eligibility; Qualifications; Number of Terms

No person shall be eligible to the Office of Governor, who is not a qualified elector, and who, at the time of such election, has not attained the age of twenty five years; and who shall not have been a citizen resident of this State for two years next preceding the election; nor shall any person be elected to the Office of Governor more than twice; and no person who has held the Office of Governor, or acted as Governor for more than two years of a term to which some other person was elected Governor shall be elected to the Office of Governor more than once.

### Section 4. Returns of General Election Transmitted to Secretary of State; Canvass by Supreme Court; Declaration of Election

The returns of every election for United States senator and member of Congress, district and state officers, and for and against any questions submitted to the electors of the State of Nevada, voted for at the general election, shall be sealed up and transmitted to the seat of government, directed to the secretary of state, and the chief justice of the supreme court, and the associate justices, or a majority thereof, shall meet at the office of the secretary of state, on a day to be fixed by law, and open and canvass the election returns for United States senator and member of Congress, district and state officers, and for and against any questions submitted to the electors of the State of Nevada, and forthwith declare the result and publish the names of the persons elected and the results of the vote cast upon any question submitted to the electors of the State of Nevada. The persons having the highest number of votes for the respective offices shall be declared elected, but in case any two or more have an equal and the highest number of votes for the same office, the legislature shall, by joint vote of both houses, elect one of said persons to fill said office.

## Section 5.   Governor is Commander in Chief of State Military Forces

The Governor shall be Commander in Chief of the Military forces of this State except when they shall be called into the service of the United States.

## Section 6.   Transaction of Executive Business; Reports of Executive Officers

He shall transact all executive business with the Officers of the Government Civil and Military; and may require information in writing, from the Officers of the Executive Department, upon any subject relating to the duties of their respective Offices.

## Section 7.   Responsibility for Execution of Laws

He shall see that the laws are faithfully executed.

## Section 8.   Vacancies Filled by Governor

When any Office shall, from any cause become vacant and no mode is provided by the Constitution and laws for filling such vacancy, the Governor shall have the power to fill such vacancy by granting a commission which shall expire at the next election and qualification of the person elected to such Office.

### Section 9. Special Sessions of Legislature: Authority of Governor; Limitations On Business and Duration; Void Actions

**1.** Except as otherwise provided in Section 2A of Article 4 of this Constitution, the Governor may, on extraordinary occasions, convene the Legislature by Proclamation and shall state to both houses, when organized, the business for which they have been specially convened.

**2.** At a special session convened pursuant to this section, the Legislature shall not introduce, consider or pass any bills except those related to the business for which the Legislature has been specially convened and those necessary to provide for the expenses of the session.

**3.** Except as otherwise provided in this subsection, the Legislature shall adjourn sine die a special session convened pursuant to this section not later than midnight Pacific time at the end of the 20th consecutive calendar day of that session, inclusive of the day on which that session commences. Any legislative action taken after midnight Pacific time at the end of the 20th consecutive calendar day of that session is void. This subsection does not apply to a special session that is convened to conduct proceedings for:

**(a)** Impeachment or removal from office of the Governor and other state and judicial officers pursuant to Article 7 of this Constitution; or

**(b)** Expulsion from office of a member of the Legislature pursuant to Section 6 of Article 4 of this Constitution.

**4.** for the purposes of this section, "midnight Pacific time" must be determined based on the actual measure of time that, on the final calendar day of the session, is being used and observed by the general population as the uniform time for the portion of Nevada which lies within the Pacific time zone, or any legal successor to the Pacific time zone, and which includes the seat of government of this State as designated by Section 1 of Article 15 of this Constitution. The Legislature and its members, officers and employees shall not employ any device, pretense or fiction that adjusts, evades or ignores this measure of time for the purpose of extending the duration of the session.

### Section 10.  Governor's Message

He shall communicate by Message to the Legislature at every regular Session the condition of the State and recommend such measures as he may deem expedient.

### Section 11.  Adjournment of Legislature by Governor

in case of a disagreement between the two Houses with respect to the time of adjournment, the Governor shall have power to adjourn the Legislature to such time as he may think proper; Provided, it be not beyond the time fixed for the meeting of the next Legislature.

### Section 12.  Person Holding Federal Office Ineligible for Office of Governor

No person shall, while holding any office under the United States Government hold the office of Governor, except as herein expressly provided.

### Section 13.  Pardons, Reprieves and Commutations of Sentence; Remission of Fines and Forfeitures

The Governor shall have the power to suspend the collection of fines and forfeitures and grant reprieves for a period not exceeding sixty days dating from the time of conviction, for all offenses, except in cases of impeachment. Upon conviction for treason he shall have power to suspend the execution of the sentence until the case shall be reported to the Legislature at its next meeting, when the Legislature shall either pardon, direct the execution of the sentence, or grant a further reprieve. and if the Legislature should fail or refuse to make final disposition of such case, the sentence shall be enforced at such time and place as the Governor by his order may direct. The Governor shall communicate to the Legislature, at the beginning of every session, every case of fine or forfeiture remitted, or reprieve, pardon, or commutation granted, stating the name of the convict, the crime of which he was convicted, the Sentence, its date, and the date of the remission, commutation, pardon or reprieve.

## Section 14.  Remission of Fines and Forfeitures; Commutations and Pardons; Suspension of Sentence; Probation

**1.**  The governor, justices of the supreme court, and attorney general, or a major part of them, of whom the governor shall be one, may, upon such conditions and with such limitations and restrictions as they may think proper, remit fines and forfeitures, commute punishments, except as provided in subsection 2, and grant pardons, after convictions, in all cases, except treason and impeachments, subject to such regulations as may be provided by law relative to the manner of applying for pardons.

**2.**  Except as may be provided by law, a sentence of death or a sentence of life imprisonment without possibility of parole may not be commuted to a sentence which would allow parole.

**3.**  The Legislature is authorized to pass laws conferring upon the district courts authority to suspend the execution of sentences, fix the conditions for, and to grant probation, and within the minimum and maximum periods authorized by law, fix the sentence to be served by the person convicted of crime in said courts.

## Section 14. State Board of Pardons Commissioners; Remission of Fines and Forfeitures; Commutations and Pardons; Suspension of Sentence; Probation

**1.** The governor, justices of the supreme court, and attorney general shall constitute the State Board of Pardons Commissioners.

**2.** The State Board of Pardons Commissioners may, upon such conditions and with such limitations and restrictions as they may think proper, remit fines and forfeitures, commute punishments, except as provided in subsection 3, and grant pardons, after convictions, in all cases, except treason and impeachments, subject to such regulations as may be provided by law relative to the manner of applying for pardons.

**3.** Except as may be provided by law, a sentence of death or a sentence of life imprisonment without possibility of parole may not be commuted to a sentence which would allow parole.

**4.** The State Board of Pardons Commissioners shall meet at least quarterly.

**5.** Any member of the State Board of Pardons Commissioners may submit matters for consideration by the State Board of Pardons Commissioners.

**6.** A majority of the members of the State Board of Pardons Commissioners is sufficient for any action taken by the State Board of Pardons Commissioners.

**7.** The Legislature is authorized to pass laws conferring upon the district courts authority to suspend the execution of sentences, fix the conditions for, and to grant probation, and within the minimum and maximum periods authorized by law, fix the sentence to be served by the person convicted of crime in said courts.

**15. The Great Seal**

There shall be a Seal of this State, which shall be kept by the Governor and used by him Officially, and shall be called "The Great Seal of the State of Nevada."

**Section 16. Grants and Commissions: Signatures and Seal**

All grants and commissions shall be in the name and by the authority of the State of Nevada, sealed with the Great Seal of the State, signed by the Governor and counter-signed by the Secretary of State.

**Section 17. Election, Term, Qualifications and Duties of Lieutenant Governor; President of Senate; President Pro-Tempore of Senate to Act as Governor in Certain Circumstances**

A Lieutenant Governor shall be elected at the same time and places and in the same manner as the Governor and his term of Office, and his eligibility, shall also be the same. He shall be President of the Senate, but shall only have a casting vote therein. If during a Vacancy of the office of Governor, the Lieutenant Governor shall be impeached, displaced, resign, die, or become incapable of performing the duties of the office, or be absent from the State, the President pro-tempore of the Senate shall act as Governor until the vacancy be filled or the disability cease.

**Section 18. Vacancy in Office of Governor; Duties to Devolve Upon Lieutenant Governor**

in case of the impeachment of the Governor, or his removal from Office, death, inability to discharge the duties of the said Office, resignation or absence from the State, the powers and duties of the Office shall devolve upon the Lieutenant Governor for the residue of the term, or until the disability shall cease. But when the Governor shall with the consent of the Legislature be out of the State, in time of War, and at the head of any military force thereof, he shall continue Commander in Chief of the military forces of the State.

## Section 19. Other State Officers: Election and Term of Office; Eligibility for Office

**1.** A Secretary of State, a Treasurer, a Controller, and an Attorney General, shall be elected at the same time and places, and in the same manner as the Governor. The term of office of each shall be the same as is prescribed for the Governor.

**2.** Any elector shall be eligible to any of these offices, but no person may be elected to any of them more than twice, or more than once if he has previously held the office by election or appointment.

## Section 20. Secretary of State: Duties

The Secretary of State shall keep a true record of the Official Acts of the Legislative and Executive Departments of the Government, and shall when required, lay the same and all matters relative thereto, before either branch of the Legislature.

## Section 21. Board of State Prison Commissioners; Board of Examiners; Examination of Claims

The Governor, Secretary of State and Attorney General shall constitute a Board of State Prison Commissioners, which Board shall have such supervision of all matters connected with the State Prison as may be provided by law. They shall also constitute a Board of Examiners, with power to examine all claims against the State (except salaries or compensation of Officers fixed by law) and perform such other duties as may be prescribed by law, and no claim against the State (except salaries or compensation of Officers fixed by law) shall be passed upon by the Legislature without having been considered and acted upon by said "Board of Examiners."

## Section 22. Duties of Certain State Officers

The Secretary of State, State Treasurer, State Controller, Attorney General, and Superintendent of Public Instruction shall perform such other duties as may be prescribed by law.

## Article VI: Judicial Department

### Section 1.  Judicial Power Vested in Court System

The judicial power of this State is vested in a court system, comprising a Supreme Court, a court of appeals, district courts and justices of the peace. The Legislature may also establish, as part of the system, courts for municipal purposes only in incorporated cities and towns.

### Section 2.  Supreme Court: Composition; Staggered Terms of Justices; Holding of Court by Panels of Justices and Full Court

**1.** The Supreme Court consists of the Chief Justice and two or more associate justices, as may be provided by law. in increasing or diminishing the number of associate justices, the Legislature shall provide for the arrangement of their terms so that an equal number of terms, as nearly as may be, expire every 2 years.

**2.** The Legislature may provide by law:

**(a)** If the Court consists of more than five justices, for the hearing and decision of cases by panels of no fewer than three justices, the resolution by the full Court of any conflicts between decisions so rendered, and the kinds of cases which must be heard by the full Court.

**(b)** for the places of holding court by panels of justices if established, and by the full Court.

### Section 3.  Justices of Supreme Court: Election; Terms; Chief Justice

The justices of the Supreme Court, shall be elected by the qualified electors of the State at the general election, and shall hold office for the term of six years from and including the first Monday of January next succeeding their election; provided, that there shall be elected, at the first election under this Constitution, three justices of the Supreme Court who shall hold office from and including the first Monday of December A.D., eighteen hundred and sixty four, and continue in office thereafter, two, four and six years respectively, from and including the first Monday of January next suceeding [succeeding] their election. They shall meet as soon as practicable after their election and qualification, and at their first meeting shall determine by lot, the term of office each shall fill, and the justice drawing the shortest term shall be Chief Justice, and after the expiration of his term, the one having the next shortest term shall be Chief Justice, after which the senior justice in commission shall be Chief Justice; and in case the commission of any two or more of said justices shall bear the same date, they shall determine by lot, who shall be Chief Justice.

**Section 3a. Court of Appeals: Composition; Panel of Judges; Appointment, Election and Terms of Judges; Chief Judge; Service of Judges as Supplemental District Judges**

**1.** The court of appeals consists of three judges or such greater number as the Legislature may provide by law. If the number of judges is so increased, the Supreme Court must provide by rule for the assignment of each appeal to a panel of three judges for decision.

**2.** After the initial terms, each judge of the court of appeals must be elected by the qualified electors of this State at the general election for a term of 6 years beginning on the first Monday of January next after the election. The initial three judges of the court of appeals must be appointed by the Governor from among three nominees selected for each individual seat by the permanent Commission on Judicial Selection described in subsection 3 of section 20 of this Article. After the expiration of 30 days from the date on which the permanent Commission on Judicial Selection has delivered to the Governor its list of nominees for the initial judges, if the

Governor has not made the appointments required by this Section, the Governor shall make no other appointment to any public office until the Governor has appointed a judge from the list submitted. The term of the initial judges is 2 years beginning on the first Monday of January next after the effective date of this Section, and an initial judge may succeed himself. If there is an increase in the number of judges, each additional judge must be elected by the qualified electors of this State at the first general election following the increase for a term of 6 years beginning on the first Monday of January next after the election.

**3.** The Chief Justice of the Supreme Court shall appoint one of the judges of the court of appeals to be chief judge. The chief judge serves a term of 4 years, except that the term of the initial chief judge is 2 years. The chief judge may succeed himself. The chief judge may resign the position of chief judge without resigning from the court of appeals.

**4.** The Supreme Court shall provide by rule for the assignment of one or more judges of the court of appeals to devote a part of their time to serve as supplemental district judges, where needed.

## Section 4. Jurisdiction of Supreme Court and Court of Appeals; Appointment of Judge to Sit for Disabled or Disqualified Justice or Judge

**1.** The Supreme Court and the court of appeals have appellate jurisdiction in all civil cases arising in district courts, and also on questions of law alone in all criminal cases in which the offense charged is within the original jurisdiction of the district courts. The Supreme Court shall fix by rule the jurisdiction of the court of appeals and shall provide for the review, where appropriate, of appeals decided by the court of appeals. The Supreme Court and the court of appeals have power to issue writs of mandamus, certiorari, prohibition, quo warranto and habeas corpus and also all writs necessary or proper to the complete exercise of their jurisdiction. Each justice of the Supreme Court and judge of the court of appeals may issue writs of habeas corpus to any part of the State, upon petition by, or on behalf of, any person held in actual custody in this State and may make such writs returnable before the issuing justice or judge or the court of which the justice or judge is a member, or before any district court in the State or any judge of a district court.

**2.** in case of the disability or disqualification, for any cause, of a justice of the Supreme Court, the Governor may designate a judge of the court of appeals or a district judge to sit in the place of the disqualified or disabled justice. The judge designated by the Governor is entitled to receive his actual expense of travel and otherwise while sitting in the Supreme Court.

**3.** in the case of the disability or disqualification, for any cause, of a judge of the court of appeals, the Governor may designate a district judge to sit in the place of the disabled or disqualified judge. The judge whom the Governor designates is entitled to receive his actual expense of travel and otherwise while sitting in the court of appeals.

### Section 5. Judicial Districts; Election and Terms of District Judges

The State is hereby divided into nine judicial districts of which the County of Storey shall constitute the First; The County of Ormsby the Second; the County of Lyon the Third; The County of Washoe the Fourth; The Counties of Nye and Churchill the Fifth; The County of Humboldt the Sixth; The County of Lander the Seventh; The County of Douglas the Eighth; and the County of Esmeralda the Ninth. The County of Roop shall be attached to the County of Washoe for judicial purposes until otherwise provided by law. The Legislature may, however, provide by law for an alteration in the boundaries or divisions of the districts herein prescribed, and also for increasing or diminishing the number of the judicial districts and judges therein. But no such change shall take effect, except in case of a vacancy, or the expiration of the term of an incumbent of the office. At the first general election under this Constitution there shall be elected in each of the respective districts (except as in this Section hereafter otherwise provided) one district judge, who shall hold office from and including the first Monday of December A.D., eighteen hundred and sixty four and until the first Monday of January in the year eighteen hundred and sixty seven. After the said first election, there shall be elected at the general election which immediately precedes the expiration of the term of his predecessor, one district judge in each of the respective judicial districts (except in the First District as in this Section hereinafter provided.) The district judges shall be elected by the qualified electors of their respective districts, and shall hold office for the term of 6 years (excepting those elected at said first election) from and including the first Monday of January, next succeeding their election and qualification; provided, that the First Judicial District shall be entitled to, and shall have three district judges, who shall possess co-extensive and concurrent jurisdiction, and who shall be elected at the same times, in the same manner, and shall hold office for the like terms as herein prescribed, in relation to the judges in other judicial districts, any one of said judges may preside on the empanneling [empaneling] of grand juries and the presentment and trial on indictments, under such rules and regulations as may be prescribed by law.

## Section 6.  District Courts: Jurisdiction; Referees; Family Court

**1.**  The District Courts in the several Judicial Districts of this State have original jurisdiction in all cases excluded by law from the original jurisdiction of justices' courts. They also have final appellate jurisdiction in cases arising in Justices Courts and such other inferior tribunals as may be established by law. The District Courts and the Judges thereof have power to issue writs of Mandamus, Prohibition, Injunction, Quo-Warranto, Certiorari, and all other writs proper and necessary to the complete exercise of their jurisdiction. The District Courts and the Judges thereof shall also have power to issue writs of Habeas Corpus on petition by, or on behalf of any person who is held in actual custody in their respective districts, or who has suffered a criminal conviction in their respective districts and has not completed the sentence imposed pursuant to the judgment of conviction.

**2.** The legislature may provide by law for:

**(a)** Referees in district courts.

**(b)** The establishment of a family court as a division of any district court and may prescribe its jurisdiction.

## Section 7. Terms of Courts

The times of holding the Supreme Court, the court of appeals and the district courts must be as fixed by law. The terms of the Supreme Court must be held at the seat of government unless the Legislature otherwise provides by law, except that the Supreme Court may hear oral argument at other places in the State. The terms of the court of appeals must be held at the place provided by law. The terms of the district courts must be held at the county seats of their respective counties unless the Legislature otherwise provides by law.

## Section 8. Number, Qualifications, Terms of Office and Jurisdiction of Justices of the Peace; Appeals; Courts of Record

**1.** The Legislature shall determine the number of justices of the peace to be elected in each city and township of the State and shall fix by law their qualifications, their terms of office and the limits of their civil and criminal jurisdiction, according to the amount in controversy, the nature of the case, the penalty provided or any combination of these.

**2.** The provisions of this section affecting the number, qualifications, terms of office and jurisdiction of justices of the peace become effective on the first Monday of January, 1979.

**3.** The Legislature shall also prescribe by law the manner, and determine the cases, in which appeals may be taken from justices and other courts. The Supreme Court, the court of appeals, the district courts and such other courts as the Legislature designates are courts of record.
Section 9. Municipal courts.

Provision shall be made by law prescribing the powers, duties and responsibilities of any Municipal Court that may be established in pursuance of Section One, of this Article; and also fixing by law the jurisdiction of said Court so as not to conflict with that of the several courts of Record.

## Section 10. Fees or Perquisites of Judicial Officers

No Judicial Officer, except Justices of the Peace and City Recorders shall receive to his own use any fees or perquisites of Office.

## Section 11. Justices and Judges Ineligible for Other Offices

The justices of the Supreme Court, the judges of the court of appeals and the district judges are ineligible to any office, other than a judicial office, during the term for which they have been elected or appointed. All elections or appointments of any such judges by the people, Legislature or otherwise during said period to any office other than judicial are void.

## Section 12. Judge not to Charge Jury Respecting Matters of Fact; Statement of Testimony and Declaration of Law

Judges shall not charge juries in respect to matters of fact, but may state the testimony and declare the law.

## Section 13. Style of Process

The style of all process shall be "The State of Nevada" and all prosecutions shall be conducted in the name and by the authority of the same.

## Section 14. One Form of Civil Action

There shall be but one form of civil action, and law and equity may be administered in the same action.

## Section 15. Compensation of Justices and Judges

The justices of the Supreme Court, the judges of the court of appeals and the district judges are each entitled to receive for their services a compensation to be fixed by law and paid in the manner provided by law, which must not be increased or diminished during the term for which they have been elected, unless a vacancy occurs, in which case the successor of the former incumbent is entitled to receive only such salary as may be provided by law at the time of his election or appointment. A provision must be made by law for setting apart from each year's revenue a sufficient amount of money to pay such compensation.

## Section 16. Special Fee in Civil Action for Compensation of Judges

The Legislature at its first Session, and from time to time thereafter shall provide by law, that upon the institution of each civil action, and other proceedings, and also upon the perfecting of an appeal in any civil action or proceeding, in the several Courts of Record in this State, a special Court fee, or tax shall be advanced to the Clerks of said Courts, respectively by the party or parties bringing such action or proceeding, or taking such appeal and the money so paid in shall be accounted for by such Clerks, and applied towards the payment of the compensation of the Judges of said Courts, as shall be directed by law.

## Section 17. Absence of Judicial Officer From State; Vacation of Office

The Legislature shall have no power to grant leave of absence to a Judicial Officer, and any such Officer who shall absent himself from the State for more than Ninety consecutive days, shall be deemed to have vacated his Office.

## Section 18. Territorial Judicial Officers Not Superseded Until Election and Qualification of Successors

No Judicial Officer shall be superceeded [superseded] nor shall the Organization of the several Courts of the Territory of Nevada be changed until the election and qualification of the several Officers provided for in this article.

## Section 19. Administration of Court System by Chief Justice

**1.** The chief justice is the administrative head of the court system. Subject to such rules as the supreme court may adopt, the chief justice may:

**(a)** Apportion the work of the supreme court among justices.

**(b)** Assign district judges to assist in other judicial districts or to specialized functions which may be established by law.

**(c)** Recall to active service any retired justice or judge of the court system who consents to such recall and who has not been removed or retired for cause or defeated for retention in office, and may assign him to appropriate temporary duty within the court system.

**2.** in the absence or temporary disability of the chief justice, the associate justice senior in commission shall act as chief justice.

**3.** This section becomes effective July 1, 1977.

**Section 20. Filling of Vacancies Occurring Before Expiration of Term of Office in Supreme Court or Court of Appeals or Among District Judges; Commission on Judicial Selection**

**1.** When a vacancy occurs before the expiration of any term of office in the Supreme Court or the court of appeals or among the district judges, the Governor shall appoint a justice or judge from among three nominees selected for such individual vacancy by the Commission on Judicial Selection.

**2.** The term of office of any justice or judge so appointed expires on the first Monday of January following the next general election.

**3.** Each nomination for the Supreme Court or the court of appeals must be made by the permanent Commission, composed of:

**(a)** The Chief Justice or an associate justice designated by him;

**(b)** Three members of the State Bar of Nevada, a public corporation created by statute, appointed by its Board of Governors; and

**(c)** Three persons, not members of the legal profession, appointed by the Governor.

**4.** Each nomination for the district court must be made by a temporary commission composed of:

**(a)** The permanent Commission;

**(b)** A member of the State Bar of Nevada resident in the judicial district in which the vacancy occurs, appointed by the Board of Governors of the State Bar of Nevada; and

**(c)** A resident of such judicial district, not a member of the legal profession, appointed by the Governor.

**5.** If at any time the State Bar of Nevada ceases to exist as a public corporation or ceases to include all attorneys admitted to practice before the courts of this State, the Legislature shall provide by law, or if it fails to do so the Supreme Court shall provide by rule, for the appointment of attorneys at law to the positions designated in this Section to be occupied by members of the State Bar of Nevada.

**6.** The term of office of each appointive member of the permanent Commission, except the first members, is 4 years. Each appointing authority shall appoint one of the members first appointed for a term of 2 years. If a vacancy occurs, the appointing authority shall fill the vacancy for the unexpired term. The additional members of a temporary commission must be appointed when a vacancy occurs, and their terms expire when the nominations for such vacancy have been transmitted to the Governor.

**7.** An appointing authority shall not appoint to the permanent Commission more than:

**(a)** One resident of any county.

**(b)** Two members of the same political party.

**(c)** No member of the permanent Commission may be a member of the Commission on Judicial Discipline.

**8.** After the expiration of 30 days from the date on which the Commission on Judicial Selection has delivered to him its list of nominees for any vacancy, if the Governor has not made the appointment required by this Section, he shall make no other appointment to any public office until he has appointed a justice or judge from the list submitted.

## Section 21. Commission on Judicial Discipline; Code of Judicial Conduct

**1.** A justice of the Supreme Court, a judge of the court of appeals, a district judge, a justice of the peace or a municipal judge may, in addition to the provision of Article 7 for impeachment, be censured, retired, removed or otherwise disciplined by the Commission on Judicial Discipline. Pursuant to rules governing appeals adopted by the Supreme Court, a justice or judge may appeal from the action of the Commission to the Supreme Court, which may reverse such action or take any alternative action provided in this subsection.

**2.** The Commission is composed of:

**(a)** Two justices or judges appointed by the Supreme Court;

**(b)** Two members of the State Bar of Nevada, a public corporation created by statute, appointed by its Board of Governors; and

**(c)** Three persons, not members of the legal profession, appointed by the Governor.

**(d)** The Commission shall elect a Chairman from among its three lay members.

**3.** If at any time the State Bar of Nevada ceases to exist as a public corporation or ceases to include all attorneys admitted to practice before the courts of this State, the Legislature shall provide by law, or if it fails to do so the Supreme Court shall provide by rule, for the appointment of attorneys at law to the positions designated in this Section to be occupied by members of the State Bar of Nevada.

**4.** The term of office of each appointive member of the Commission, except the first members, is 4 years. Each appointing authority shall appoint one of the members first appointed for a term of 2 years. If a vacancy occurs, the appointing authority shall fill the vacancy for the unexpired term. An appointing authority shall not appoint more than one resident of any county. The Governor shall not appoint more than two members of the same political party. No member may be a member of a commission on judicial selection.

**5.** The Legislature shall establish:

**(a)** in addition to censure, retirement and removal, the other forms of disciplinary action that the Commission may impose;

**(b)** The grounds for censure and other disciplinary action that the Commission may impose, including, but not limited to, violations of the provisions of the Code of Judicial Conduct;

**(c)** The standards for the investigation of matters relating to the fitness of a justice or judge; and

**(d)** The confidentiality or nonconfidentiality, as appropriate, of proceedings before the Commission, except that, in any event, a decision to censure, retire or remove a justice or judge must be made public.

**6.** The Supreme Court shall adopt a Code of Judicial Conduct.

**7.** The Commission shall adopt rules of procedure for the conduct of its hearings and any other procedural rules it deems necessary to carry out its duties.

**8.** No justice or judge may by virtue of this Section be:

**(a)** Removed except for willful misconduct, willful or persistent failure to perform the duties of his office or habitual intemperance; or

**(b)** Retired except for advanced age which interferes with the proper performance of his judicial duties, or for mental or physical disability which prevents the proper performance of his judicial duties and which is likely to be permanent in nature.

**9.** Any matter relating to the fitness of a justice or judge may be brought to the attention of the Commission by any person or on the motion of the Commission. The Commission shall, after preliminary investigation, dismiss the matter or order a hearing to be held before it. If a hearing is ordered, a statement of the matter must be served upon the justice or judge against whom the proceeding is brought. The Commission in its discretion may suspend a justice or judge from the exercise of his office pending the determination of the proceedings before the Commission. Any justice or judge whose removal is sought is liable to indictment and punishment according to law. A justice or judge retired for disability in accordance with this Section is entitled thereafter to receive such compensation as the Legislature may provide.

**10.** If a proceeding is brought against a justice of the Supreme Court, no justice of the Supreme Court may sit on the Commission for that proceeding. If a proceeding is brought against a judge of the court of appeals, no judge of the court of appeals may sit on the Commission for that proceeding. If a proceeding is brought against a district judge, no district judge from the same judicial district may sit on the Commission for that proceeding. If a proceeding is brought against a justice of the peace, no justice of the peace from the same township may sit on the Commission for that proceeding. If a proceeding is brought against a municipal judge, no municipal judge from the same city may sit on the Commission for that proceeding. If an appeal is taken from an action of the Commission to the Supreme Court, any justice who sat on the Commission for that proceeding is disqualified from participating in the consideration or decision of the appeal. When any member of the Commission is disqualified by this subsection, the Supreme Court shall appoint a substitute from among the eligible judges.

**11.** The Commission may:

**(a)** Designate for each hearing an attorney or attorneys at law to act as counsel to conduct the proceeding;

**(b)** Summon witnesses to appear and testify under oath and compel the production of books, papers, documents and records;

**(c)** Grant immunity from prosecution or punishment when the Commission deems it necessary and proper in order to compel the giving of testimony under oath and the production of books, papers, documents and records; and

**(d)** Exercise such further powers as the Legislature may from time to time confer upon it.

## Article VII: Impeachment and Removal from Office

### Section. 1. Impeachment: Trial; Conviction

The Assembly shall have the sole power of impeaching. The concurrence of a majority of all the members elected, shall be necessary to an impeachment. All impeachments shall be tried by the Senate, and when sitting for that purpose, the Senators shall be upon Oath or Affirmation, to do justice according to Law and Evidence. The Chief Justice of the Supreme court, shall preside over the Senate while sitting to try the Governor or Lieutenant Governor upon impeachment. No person shall be convicted without the concurrence of two thirds of the Senators elected.

### Section 2. Officers Subject to Impeachment

The Governor and other state and judicial officers, except justices of the peace shall be liable to impeachment for misdemeanor or malfeasance in office; but judgment in such case shall not extend further than removal from office and disqualification to hold any office of honor, profit, or trust under this State. The party whether convicted or acquitted, shall, nevertheless, be liable to indictment, trial, judgment and punishment according to law.

### Section 3. Removal of Justices of Supreme Court, Judges of Court of Appeals and Judges of District Courts

for any reasonable cause to be entered on the journals of each House, which may or may not be sufficient grounds for impeachment, the justices of the Supreme Court, the judges of the court of appeals and the judges of the district courts must be removed from office on the vote of two thirds of the members elected to each branch of the Legislature. The justice or judge complained of must be served with a copy of the complaint against him, and have an opportunity of being heard in person or by counsel in his defense. No member of either branch of the

Legislature is eligible to fill the vacancy occasioned by such removal.

## Section 4.  Removal of Other Civil Officers

Provision shall be made by law for the removal from Office of any Civil Officer other than those in this Article previously specified, for Malfeasance, or Nonfeasance in the Performance of his duties.

## Article VIII: Municipal and Other Corporations

### Section 1.   Corporations Formed Under General Laws; Municipal Corporations Formed Under Special Acts

The Legislature shall pass no Special Act in any manner relating to corporate powers except for Municipal purposes; but corporations may be formed under general laws; and all such laws may from time to time, be altered or repealed.

### Section 2.   Corporate Property Subject to Taxation; Exemptions

All real property, and possessory rights to the same, as well as personal property in this State, belonging to corporations now existing or hereafter created shall be subject to taxation, the same as property of individuals; Provided, that the property of corporations formed for Municipal, Charitable, Religious, or Educational purposes may be exempted by law.

### Section 3.   Individual Liability of Corporators

Dues from corporations shall be secured by such means as may be prescribed by law; Provided, that corporators in corporations formed under the laws of this State shall not be individually liable for the debts or liabilities of such corporation.

### Section 4.   Regulation of Corporations Incorporated Under Territorial Law

Corporations created by or under the laws of the Territory of Nevada shall be subject to the provisions of such laws until the Legislature shall pass laws regulating the same, in pursuance of the provisions of this Constitution.

## Section 5. Corporations May Sue and be Sued

Corporations may sue and be sued in all courts, in like manner as individuals.

## Section 6. Circulation of Certain Bank Notes or Paper as Money Prohibited

No bank notes or paper of any kind shall ever be permitted to circulate as money in this State, except the Federal currency, and the notes of banks authorized under the laws of Congress.

## Section 7. Eminent Domain by Corporations

No right of way shall be appropriated to the use of any corporation until full compensation be first made or secured therefor.

## Section 8. Municipal Corporations Formed Under General Laws

The legislature shall provide for the organization of cities and towns by general laws and shall restrict their power of taxation, assessment, borrowing money, contracting debts and loaning their credit, except for procuring supplies of water; provided, however, that the legislature may, by general laws, in the manner and to the extent therein provided, permit and authorize the electors of any city or town to frame, adopt and amend a charter for its own government, or to amend any existing charter of such city or town.

## Section 9. Gifts or Loans of Public Money to Certain Corporations Prohibited

The State shall not donate or loan money, or its credit, subscribe to or be, interested in the Stock of any company, association, or corporation, except corporations formed for educational or charitable purposes.

**Section 10. Loans of Public Money to or Ownership of Stock in Certain Corporations by County or Municipal Corporation Prohibited**

No county, city, town, or other municipal corporation shall become a stockholder in any joint stock company, corporation or association whatever, or loan its credit in aid of any such company, corporation or association, except, rail-road corporations, companies or associations.

## Article IX: Finance and State Debt

### Section 1. Fiscal Year

The fiscal year shall commence on the first day of July of each year.

### Section 2. Annual Tax for State Expenses; Trust Funds for Industrial Accidents, Occupational Diseases and Public Employees' Retirement System; Administration of Public Employees' Retirement System

**1.** The legislature shall provide by law for an annual tax sufficient to defray the estimated expenses of the state for each fiscal year; and whenever the expenses of any year exceed the income, the legislature shall provide for levying a tax sufficient, with other sources of income, to pay the deficiency, as well as the estimated expenses of such ensuing year or two years.

**2.** Any money paid for the purpose of providing compensation for industrial accidents and occupational diseases, and for administrative expenses incidental thereto, and for the purpose of funding and administering a public employees' retirement system, must be segregated in proper accounts in the state treasury, and such money must never be used for any other purposes, and they are hereby declared to be trust funds for the uses and purposes herein specified.

**3.** Any money paid for the purpose of funding and administering a public employees' retirement system must not be loaned to the state or invested to purchase any obligations of the state.

**4.** The public employees' retirement system must be governed by a public employees' retirement board. The board shall employ an executive officer who serves at the pleasure of the board. in addition to any other employees authorized by the board, the board shall employ an independent actuary. The board shall adopt actuarial assumptions based upon the recommendations made by the independent actuary it employs.

### Sec. 3.   State Indebtedness: Limitations and Exceptions

The State may contract public debts; but such debts shall never, in the aggregate, exclusive of interest, exceed the sum of two per cent of the assessed valuation of the State, as shown by the reports of the county assessors to the State Controller, except for the purpose of defraying extraordinary expenses, as hereinafter mentioned. Every such debt shall be authorized by law for some purpose or purposes, to be distinctly specified therein; and every such law shall provide for levying an annual tax sufficient to pay the interest semiannually, and the principal within twenty years from the passage of such law, and shall specially appropriate the proceeds of said taxes to the payment of said principal and interest; and such appropriation shall not be repealed nor the taxes postponed or diminished until the principal and interest of said debts shall have been wholly paid. Every contract of indebtedness entered into or assumed by or on behalf of the State, when all its debts and liabilities amount to said sum before mentioned, shall be void and of no effect, except in cases of money borrowed to repel invasion, suppress insurrection, defend the State in time of war, or, if hostilities be threatened, provide for the public defense.

The State, notwithstanding the foregoing limitations, may, pursuant to authority of the Legislature, make and enter into any and all contracts necessary, expedient or advisable for the protection and preservation of any of its property or natural resources, or for the purposes of obtaining the benefits thereof, however arising and whether arising by or through any undertaking or project of the United States or by or through any treaty or compact between the states, or otherwise. The Legislature may from time to time make such appropriations as may be necessary to carry out the obligations of the State under such contracts, and shall levy such tax as may be necessary to pay the same or carry them into effect.

## Section 4. Assumption of Debts of County, City or Corporation by State

The State shall never assume the debts of any county, town, city or other corporation whatever, unless such debts have been created to repel invasion, suppress insurrection or to provide for the public defense.

## Section 5. Proceeds From Fees for Licensing and Registration of Motor Vehicles and Excise Taxes On Fuel Reserved for Construction, Maintenance and Repair of Public Highways; Exception

The proceeds from the imposition of any license or registration fee and other charge with respect to the operation of any motor vehicle upon any public highway in this State and the proceeds from the imposition of any excise tax on gasoline or other motor vehicle fuel shall, except costs of administration, be used exclusively for the construction, maintenance, and repair of the public highways of this State. The provisions of this section do not apply to the proceeds of any tax imposed upon motor vehicles by the Legislature in lieu of an ad valorem property tax.

## Article X: Taxation

## Section 1. Uniform and Equal Rate of Assessment and Taxation; Valuation of Property; Exceptions and Exemptions; Inheritance and Personal Income Taxes Prohibited

**1.** The Legislature shall provide by law for a uniform and equal rate of assessment and taxation, and shall prescribe such regulations as shall secure a just valuation for taxation of all property, real, personal and possessory, except mines and mining claims, which shall be assessed and taxed only as provided in Section 5 of this Article.

**2.** Shares of stock, bonds, mortgages, notes, bank deposits, book accounts and credits, and securities and choses in action of like character are deemed to represent interest in property already assessed and taxed, either in Nevada or elsewhere, and shall be exempt.

**3.** The Legislature may constitute agricultural and open-space real property having a greater value for another use than that for which it is being used, as a separate class for taxation purposes and may provide a separate uniform plan for appraisal and valuation of such property for assessment purposes. If such plan is provided, the Legislature shall also provide for retroactive assessment for a period of not less than 7 years when agricultural and open-space real property is converted to a higher use conforming to the use for which other nearby property is used.

**4.** Personal property which is moving in interstate commerce through or over the territory of the State of Nevada, or which was consigned to a warehouse, public or private, within the State of Nevada from outside the State of Nevada for storage in transit to a final destination outside the State of Nevada, whether specified when transportation begins or afterward, shall be deemed to have acquired no situs in Nevada for purposes of taxation and shall be exempt from taxation. Such property shall not be deprived of such exemption because while in the warehouse the property is assembled, bound, joined, processed, disassembled, divided, cut, broken in bulk, relabeled or repackaged.

**5.** The Legislature may exempt motor vehicles from the provisions of the tax required by this Section, and in lieu thereof, if such exemption is granted, shall provide for a uniform and equal rate of assessment and taxation of motor vehicles, which rate shall not exceed five cents on one dollar of assessed valuation.

**6.** The Legislature shall provide by law for a progressive reduction in the tax upon business inventories by 20 percent in each year following the adoption of this provision, and after the expiration of the 4th year such inventories are exempt from taxation. The Legislature may exempt any other personal property, including livestock.

**7.** No inheritance tax shall ever be levied.

**8.** The Legislature may exempt by law property used for municipal, educational, literary, scientific or other charitable purposes, or to encourage the conservation of energy or the substitution of other sources for fossil sources of energy.

**9.** No income tax shall be levied upon the wages or personal income of natural persons. Notwithstanding the foregoing provision, and except as otherwise provided in subsection 1 of this Section, taxes may be levied upon the income or revenue of any business in whatever form it may be conducted for profit in the State.

**10.** The Legislature may provide by law for an abatement of the tax upon or an exemption of part of the assessed value of a single-family residence occupied by the owner to the extent necessary to avoid severe economic hardship to the owner of the residence.

## Section 1.  Uniform and Equal Rate of Assessment and Taxation; Valuation of Property; Exceptions and Exemptions; Inheritance and Personal Income Taxes Prohibited; Program for Refunds of Property Taxes to Seniors and Persons with Disabilities

**1.**  The Legislature shall provide by law for a uniform and equal rate of assessment and taxation, and shall prescribe such regulations as shall secure a just valuation for taxation of all property, real, personal and possessory, except mines and mining claims, which shall be assessed and taxed only as provided in Section 5 of this Article.

**2.**  Shares of stock, bonds, mortgages, notes, bank deposits, book accounts and credits, and securities and choses in action of like character are deemed to represent interest in property already assessed and taxed, either in Nevada or elsewhere, and shall be exempt.

**3.**  The Legislature may constitute agricultural and open-space real property having a greater value for another use than that for which it is being used, as a separate class for taxation purposes and may provide a separate uniform plan for appraisal and valuation of such property for assessment purposes. If such plan is provided, the Legislature shall also provide for retroactive assessment for a period of not less than 7 years when agricultural and open-space real property is converted to a higher use conforming to the use for which other nearby property is used.

**4.**  Personal property which is moving in interstate commerce through or over the territory of the State of Nevada, or which was consigned to a warehouse, public or private, within the State of Nevada from outside the State of Nevada for storage in transit to a final destination outside the State of Nevada, whether specified when transportation begins or afterward, shall be deemed to have acquired no situs in Nevada for purposes of taxation and shall be exempt from taxation. Such property shall not be deprived of such exemption because while in the warehouse the property is assembled, bound, joined, processed, disassembled, divided, cut, broken in bulk, relabeled or repackaged.

**5.** The Legislature may exempt motor vehicles from the provisions of the tax required by this Section, and in lieu thereof, if such exemption is granted, shall provide for a uniform and equal rate of assessment and taxation of motor vehicles, which rate shall not exceed five cents on one dollar of assessed valuation.

**6.** The Legislature shall provide by law for a progressive reduction in the tax upon business inventories by 20 percent in each year following the adoption of this provision, and after the expiration of the 4th year such inventories are exempt from taxation. The Legislature may exempt any other personal property, including livestock.

**7.** No inheritance tax shall ever be levied.

**8.** The Legislature may exempt by law property used for municipal, educational, literary, scientific or other charitable purposes, or to encourage the conservation of energy or the substitution of other sources for fossil sources of energy

**9.** No income tax shall be levied upon the wages or personal income of natural persons. Notwithstanding the foregoing provision, and except as otherwise provided in subsection 1 of this Section, taxes may be levied upon the income or revenue of any business in whatever form it may be conducted for profit in the State.

**10.** The Legislature may provide by law for an abatement of the tax upon or an exemption of part of the assessed value of a single-family residence occupied by the owner to the extent necessary to avoid severe economic hardship to the owner of the residence.

**11.** for the purposes of assessment and taxation of property:

**(a)** Except as otherwise provided in this paragraph, for the first fiscal year after the sale or transfer of real property, the real property sold or transferred shall not be eligible for any adjustment provided by the Legislature by law based on the age of improvements to the real property, any abatement of the tax upon the real property provided by the Legislature by law pursuant to subsection 8 or any abatement or exemption provided by the Legislature by law pursuant to subsection 10. The provisions of this paragraph do not apply to real property for which the Legislature has provided by law for an exemption of the tax on property.

**(b)** for any fiscal year following the first fiscal year after the sale or transfer of real property to which the provisions of paragraph (a) apply, any adjustment provided by the Legislature by law based on the age of improvements to the real property must be determined as if the improvements were new improvements on the date of the sale or transfer.
Ê The Legislature shall provide by law for definitions of the terms "sale" and "transfer" as necessary to carry out the provisions of this subsection.

**12.** The Legislature shall provide by law for a program to provide for the payment of refunds of the taxes imposed on the primary residence of a person domiciled in this State who is 62 years of age or older or a person with a disability. If such a person rents his or her primary residence, the amount of the refund for which the person is eligible must not exceed the portion of the rent which is deemed to constitute accrued property tax. The Legislature shall establish by law:

**(a)** The criteria which a person must satisfy to be eligible for such a refund; and

**(b)** The amount of the refund to be paid to a person eligible for such a refund, which may consist of a graduated refund based on the household income of such a person.

## Section 2. Total Tax Levy for Public Purposes Limited

The total tax levy for all public purposes including levies for bonds, within the state, or any subdivision thereof, shall not exceed five cents on one dollar of assessed valuation.

## Section 3. Household Goods and Furniture of Single Household Exempt from Taxation

All household goods and furniture used by a single household and owned by a member of that household are exempt from taxation.

## Section 3a. Food Exempt from Taxes On Retail Sales; Exceptions

The legislature shall provide by law for:

**1.** The exemption of food for human consumption from any tax upon the sale, storage, use or consumption of tangible personal property; and

**2.** These commodities to be excluded from any such exemption:

**(a)** Prepared food intended for immediate consumption.

**(b)** Alcoholic beverages.

**3b.** Durable medical equipment, oxygen delivery equipment and mobility enhancing equipment exempt from taxes on retail sales.

## Section 4. Taxation of Estates Taxed by United States; Limitations

The legislature may provide by law for the taxation of estates taxed by the United States, but only to the extent of any credit allowed by federal law for the payment of the state tax and only for the purpose of education, to be divided between the common schools and the state university for their support and maintenance. The combined amount of these federal and state taxes may not exceed the estate tax which would be imposed by federal law alone. If another state of the United States imposes and collects death taxes against an estate which is taxable by the State of Nevada under this section, the amount of estate tax to be collected by the State of Nevada must be reduced by the amount of the death taxes collected by the other state. Any lien for the estate tax attaches no sooner than the time when the tax is due and payable, and no restriction on possession or use of a decedent's property may be imposed by law before the time when the tax is due and payable in full under federal law. The State of Nevada shall:

**1.** Accept the determination by the United States of the amount of the taxable estate without further audit.

**2.** Accept payment of the tax in installments proportionate to any which may be permitted under federal law.

**3.** Impose no penalty for such a deferred payment.

**4.** Not charge interest on a deferred or belated payment at any rate higher than may be provided in similar circumstances by federal law.

## Section 5. Tax On Proceeds of Minerals; Appropriation to Counties; Apportionment; Assessment and Taxation of Mines

**1.** The legislature shall provide by law for a tax upon the net proceeds of all minerals, including oil, gas and other hydrocarbons, extracted in this state, at a rate not to exceed 5 percent of the net proceeds. No other tax may be imposed upon a mineral or its proceeds until the identity of the proceeds as such is lost.

**2.** The legislature shall appropriate to each county that sum which would be produced by levying a tax upon the entire amount of the net proceeds taxed in each taxing district in the county at the rate levied in that district upon the assessed valuation of real property. The total amount so appropriated to each county must be apportioned among the respective governmental units and districts within it, including the county itself and the school district, in the same proportion as they share in the total taxes collected on property according to value.

**3.** Each patented mine or mining claim must be assessed and taxed as other real property is assessed and taxed, except that no value may be attributed to any mineral known or believed to underlie it, and no value may be attributed to the surface of a mine or claim if one hundred dollars' worth of labor has been actually performed on the mine or claim during the year preceding the assessment.

## Section 6. Enactment of Exemption from Ad Valorem Tax On Property or Excise Tax On Retail Sales

**1.** The Legislature shall not enact an exemption from any ad valorem tax on property or excise tax on the sale, storage, use or consumption of tangible personal property sold at retail unless the Legislature finds that the exemption:

**(a)** Will achieve a bona fide social or economic purpose and the benefits of the exemption are expected to exceed any adverse effect of the exemption on the provision of services to the public by the State or a local government that would otherwise receive revenue from the tax from which the exemption would be granted; and

**(b)** Will not impair adversely the ability of the State or a local government to pay, when due, all interest and principal on any outstanding bonds or any other obligations for which revenue from the tax from which the exemption would be granted was pledged.

**2.** in enacting an exemption from any ad valorem tax on property or excise tax on the sale, storage, use or consumption of tangible personal property sold at retail, the Legislature shall:

**(a)** Ensure that the requirements for claiming the exemption are as similar as practicable for similar classes of taxpayers; and

**(b)** Provide a specific date on which the exemption will cease to be effective.

## Article XI: Education

### Section 1. Legislature to Encourage Education; Appointment, Term and Duties of Superintendent of Public Instruction

The legislature shall encourage by all suitable means the promotion of intellectual, literary, scientific, mining, mechanical, agricultural, and moral improvements, and also provide for a superintendent of public instruction and by law prescribe the manner of appointment, term of office and the duties thereof.

### Section 2. Uniform System of Common Schools

The legislature shall provide for a uniform system of common schools, by which a school shall be established and maintained in each school district at least six months in every year, and any school district which shall allow instruction of a sectarian character therein may be deprived of its proportion of the interest of the public school fund during such neglect or infraction, and the legislature may pass such laws as will tend to secure a general attendance of the children in each school district upon said public schools.

### Section 3. Pledge of Certain Property and Money, Escheated Estates and Fines Collected Under Penal Laws for Educational Purposes; Apportionment and Use of Interest

All lands granted by Congress to this state for educational purposes, all estates that escheat to the state, all property given or bequeathed to the state for educational purposes, and the proceeds derived from these sources, together with that percentage of the proceeds from the sale of federal lands which has been granted by Congress to this state without restriction or for educational purposes and all fines collected under the penal laws of the state are hereby pledged for educational purposes and the money therefrom must not be transferred to other funds for other uses. The interest only earned on the money derived from these sources must be apportioned by the legislature among the several counties for educational purposes, and, if necessary, a portion of that interest may be appropriated for the support of the state university, but any of that interest which is unexpended at the end of any year must be added to the principal sum pledged for educational purposes.

## Section 4. Establishment of State University; Legislature to Provide by Law for Governance, Control and Management of State University and Protection of Academic Freedom

**1.** The Legislature shall provide for the establishment of a State University which shall embrace departments for Agriculture, Mechanic Arts, and Mining, and other departments deemed appropriate for the State University.

**2.** The Legislature shall provide by law for:

**(a)** The governance, control and management of the State University.

**(b)** The reasonable protection of individual academic freedom for persons who are enrolled in or who are employees or contractors of the State University and other public institutions of higher education in this State in order to facilitate the policies of Section 1 of this Article to encourage by all suitable means the promotion of intellectual, literary, scientific, mining, mechanical, agricultural, ethical and other educational improvements.

## Section 5. Establishment of Normal Schools and Grades of Schools; Oath of Teachers and Professors

The Legislature shall have power to establis [establish] Normal schools, and such different grades of schools, from the primary department to the University, as in their discretion they may deem necessary, and all Professors in said University, or Teachers in said Schools of whatever grade, shall be required to take and subscribe to the oath as prescribed in Article Fifteenth of this Constitution. No Professor or Teacher who fails to comply with the provisions of any law framed in accordance with the provisions of this Section, shall be entitled to receive any portion of the public monies set apart for school purposes.

### Section 6. Support of University and Common Schools by Direct Legislative Appropriation; Priority of Appropriations

**1.** in addition to other means provided for the support and maintenance of said university and common schools, the legislature shall provide for their support and maintenance by direct legislative appropriation from the general fund, upon the presentation of budgets in the manner required by law.

**2.** During a regular session of the Legislature, before any other appropriation is enacted to fund a portion of the state budget for the next ensuing biennium, the Legislature shall enact one or more appropriations to provide the money the Legislature deems to be sufficient, when combined with the local money reasonably available for this purpose, to fund the operation of the public schools in the State for kindergarten through grade 12 for the next ensuing biennium for the population reasonably estimated for that biennium.

**3.** During a special session of the Legislature that is held between the end of a regular session in which the Legislature has not enacted the appropriation or appropriations required by subsection 2 to fund education for the next ensuing biennium and the first day of that next ensuing biennium, before any other appropriation is enacted other than appropriations required to pay the cost of that special session, the Legislature shall enact one or more appropriations to provide the money the Legislature deems to be sufficient, when combined with the local money reasonably available for this purpose, to fund the operation of the public schools in the State for kindergarten through grade 12 for the next ensuing biennium for the population reasonably estimated for that biennium.

**4.** During a special session of the Legislature that is held in a biennium for which the Legislature has not enacted the appropriation or appropriations required by subsection 2 to fund education for the biennium in which the special session is being held, before any other appropriation is enacted other than appropriations required to pay the cost of that special session, the Legislature shall enact one or more appropriations to provide the money the Legislature deems to be sufficient, when combined with the local money reasonably available for this purpose, to fund the operation of the public schools in the State for kindergarten through grade 12 for the population reasonably estimated for the biennium in which the special session is held.

**5.** Any appropriation of money enacted in violation of subsection 2, 3 or 4 is void.

**6.** as used in this section, "biennium" means a period of two fiscal years beginning on July 1 of an odd-numbered year and ending on June 30 of the next ensuing odd-numbered year.

### Section 7. Board of Regents: Election and Duties

The Governor, Secretary of State, and Superintendent of Public Instruction, shall for the first four years and until their successors are elected and qualified constitute a Board of Regents to control and manage the affairs of the University and the funds of the same under such regulations as may be provided by law. But the Legislature shall at its regular session next preceding the expiration of the term of office of said Board of Regents provide for the election of a new Board of Regents and define their duties.

## Section 8. Immediate Organization and Maintenance of State University

The Board of Regents shall, from the interest accruing from the first funds which come under their control, immediately organize and maintain the said Mining department in such manner as to make it most effective and useful, Provided, that all the proceeds of the public lands donated by Act of Congress approved July second AD. Eighteen hundred and sixty Two, for a college for the benefit of Agriculture, the Mechanics Arts, and including Military tactics shall be invested by the said Board of Regents in a separate fund to be appropriated exclusively for the benefit of the first named departments to the University as set forth in Section Four above; and the Legislature shall provide that if through neglect or any other contingency, any portion of the fund so set apart, shall be lost or misappropriated, the State of Nevada shall replace said amount so lost or misappropriated in said fund so that the principal of said fund shall remain forever undiminished.

## Section 9. Sectarian Instruction Prohibited in Common Schools and University

No sectarian instruction shall be imparted or tolerated in any school or University that may be established under this Constitution.

## Section Ten. No Public Money to be Used for Sectarian Purposes

No public funds of any kind or character whatever, State, County or Municipal, shall be used for sectarian purpose.

## Article XII: Militia

### Section 1. Legislature to Provide for Militia

The Legislature shall provide by law for organizing and disciplining the Militia of this State, for the effectual encouragement of Volunteer Corps and the safe keeping of the public Arms.

### Section 2. Power of Governor to Call Out Militia

The Governor shall have power to call out the Militia to execute the laws of the State or to suppress insurrection or repel invasion.

## Article XIII: Public Institutions

### Section. 1. Institutions for Insane, Blind, Deaf and Dumb to be Fostered and Supported by State

Institutions for the benefit of the Insane, Blind and Deaf and Dumb, and such other benevolent institutions as the public good may require, shall be fostered and supported by the State, subject to such regulations as may be prescribed by law.

### Sec: 2. State Prison: Establishment and Maintenance; Juvenile Offenders

A State Prison shall be established and maintained in such manner as may be prescribed by law, and provision may be made by law for the establishment and maintainance [maintenance] of a House of Refuge for Juvenile Offenders.

### Sec: 3. County Public Welfare

Repealed.

## Article XIV: Boundary

### Section. 1. Boundary of the State of Nevada

The boundary of the State of Nevada is as follows:

Commencing at a point formed by the intersection of the forty-third degree of longitude West from Washington with the forty-second degree of North latitude; thence due East along the forty-second degree of North latitude to its intersection with the thirty-seventh degree of longitude West from Washington; thence South on the thirty-seventh degree of longitude West from Washington to its intersection with the middle line of the Colorado River of the West; thence down the middle line of the Colorado River of the West to its intersection with the Eastern boundary of the State of California; thence in a North Westerly direction along the Eastern boundary line of the State of California to the forty-third degree of Longitude West from Washington; Thence North along the forty-third degree of West Longitude, and the Eastern boundary line of the State of California to the place of beginning. All territory lying West of and adjoining the boundary line herein prescribed, which the State of California may relinquish to the Territory or State of Nevada, shall thereupon be embraced within and constitute a part of this State.

## Article XV: Miscellaneous Provisions

### Section 1. Carson City Seat of Government

The seat of Government shall be at Carson City, but no appropriation for the erection or purchase of Capitol buildings shall be made during the next three Years.

### Section 2. Oath of Office

Members of the legislature, and all officers, executive, judicial and ministerial, shall, before they enter upon the duties of their respective offices, take and subscribe to the following oath:

I, ................, do solemly [solemnly] swear (or affirm) that I will support, protect and defend the constitution and government of the United States, and the constitution and government of the State of Nevada, against all enemies, whether domestic or foreign, and that I will bear true faith, allegiance and loyalty to the same, any ordinance, resolution or law of any state notwithstanding, and that I will well and faithfully perform all the duties of the office of ................, on which I am about to enter; (if an oath) so help me God; (if an affirmation) under the pains and penalties of perjury.

### Section 3. Eligibility for Public Office

**1.** No person shall be eligible to any office who is not a qualified elector under this Constitution.

**2.** No person may be elected to any state office or local governing body who has served in that office, or at the expiration of his current term if he is so serving will have served, 12 years or more, unless the permissible number of terms or duration of service is otherwise specified in this Constitution.

## Sec: 4. Perpetuities; Eleemosynary Purposes

No perpetuities shall be allowed except for eleemosynary purposes.

## Section 5. Time of General Election

The general election shall be held on the Tuesday next after the first Monday of November.

## Section 6. Number of Members of Legislature Limited

The aggregate number of members of both branches of the Legislature shall never exceed Seventy five.

## Section 7. County Offices At County Seats

All county Officers shall hold their Offices at the County seat of their respective Counties.

## Section 8. Publication of General Statutes; Publication and Effective Date of Decisions of Supreme Court and Court of Appeals

The Legislature shall provide for the speedy publication of all statute laws of a general nature and such decisions of the Supreme Court and the court of appeals as it may deem expedient. All laws and judicial decisions must be free for publication by any person. No judgment of the Supreme Court or the court of appeals shall take effect and be operative until the opinion of the court in such case is filed with the clerk of said court.

## Section 9. Increase or Decrease of Compensation of Officers Whose Compensation Fixed by Constitution

The Legislature may, at any time, provide by law for increasing or diminishing the salaries or compensation of any of the Officers, whose salaries or compensation is fixed in this Constitution; Provided, no such change of Salary or compensation shall apply to any Officer during the term for which he may have been elected.

## Section 10. Election or Appointment of Officers

All officers whose election or appointment is not otherwise provided for, shall be chosen or appointed as may be prescribed by law.

## Section 11. Term of Office When Not Fixed by Constitution; Limitation; Municipal Officers and Employees

The tenure of any office not herein provided for may be declared by law, or, when not so declared, such office shall be held during the pleasure of the authority making the appointment, but the Legislature shall not create any office the tenure of which shall be longer than four (4) years, except as herein otherwise provided in this Constitution. in the case of any officer or employee of any municipality governed under a legally adopted charter, the provisions of such charter with reference to the tenure of office or the dismissal from office of any such officer or employee shall control.

## Section 12. Certain State Officers to Keep Offices At Carson City

The Governor, Secretary of State, State Treasurer, State Controller, and Clerk of the Supreme Court, shall keep their respective offices at the seat of Government.

## Section 13. Census by Legislature and Congress: Basis of Representation in Houses of Legislature

The enumeration of the inhabitants of this State shall be taken under the direction of the Legislature if deemed necessary in AD Eighteen hundred and Sixty five, AD Eighteen hundred and Sixty seven, AD Eighteen hundred and Seventy five, and every ten years thereafter; and these enumerations, together with the census that may be taken under the direction of the Congress of the United States in A.D. Eighteen hundred and Seventy, and every subsequent ten years shall serve as the basis of representation in both houses of the Legislature.

## Section 14. Election by Plurality

A plurality of votes given at an election by the people, shall constitute a choice, where not otherwise provided by this Constitution.

## Section 15. Merit System Governing Employment in Executive Branch of State Government

The legislature shall provide by law for a state merit system governing the employment of employees in the executive branch of state government.

## Section 16. Payment of Minimum Compensation to Employees

**A.** Each employer shall pay a wage to each employee of not less than the hourly rates set forth in this section. The rate shall be five dollars and fifteen cents ($5.15) per hour worked, if the employer provides health benefits as described herein, or six dollars and fifteen cents ($6.15) per hour if the employer does not provide such benefits. Offering health benefits within the meaning of this section shall consist of making health insurance available to the employee for the employee and the employee's dependents at a total cost to the employee for premiums of not more than 10 percent of the employee's gross taxable income from the employer. These rates of wages shall be adjusted by the amount of increases in the federal minimum wage over $5.15 per hour, or, if greater, by the cumulative increase in the cost of living. The cost of living increase shall be measured by the percentage increase as of December 31 in any year over the level as of December 31, 2004 of the Consumer Price Index (All Urban Consumers, U.S. City Average) as published by the Bureau of Labor Statistics, U.S. Department of Labor or the successor index or federal agency. No CPI adjustment for any one-year period may be greater than 3%. The Governor or the State agency designated by the Governor shall publish a bulletin by April 1 of each year announcing the adjusted rates, which shall take effect the following July 1. Such bulletin will be made available to all employers and to any other person who has filed with the Governor or the designated agency a request to receive such notice but lack of notice shall not excuse noncompliance with this section. An employer shall provide written notification of the rate adjustments to each of its employees and make the necessary payroll adjustments by July 1 following the publication of the bulletin. Tips or gratuities received by employees shall not be credited as being any part of or offset against the wage rates required by this section.

**B.** The provisions of this section may not be waived by agreement between an individual employee and an employer. All of the provisions of this section, or any part hereof, may be waived in a bona fide collective bargaining agreement, but only if the waiver is explicitly set forth in such agreement in clear and unambiguous terms. Unilateral implementation of terms and conditions of employment by either party to a collective bargaining relationship shall not constitute, or be permitted, as a waiver of all or any part of the provisions of this section. An employer shall not discharge, reduce the compensation of or otherwise discriminate against any employee for using any civil remedies to enforce this section or otherwise asserting his or her rights under this section. An employee claiming violation of this section may bring an action against his or her employer in the courts of this State to enforce the provisions of this section and shall be entitled to all remedies available under the law or in equity appropriate to remedy any violation of this section, including but not limited to back pay, damages, reinstatement or injunctive relief. An employee who prevails in any action to enforce this section shall be awarded his or her reasonable attorney's fees and costs.

**C.** as used in this section, "employee" means any person who is employed by an employer as defined herein but does not include an employee who is under eighteen (18) years of age, employed by a nonprofit organization for after school or summer employment or as a trainee for a period not longer than ninety (90) days. "Employer" means any individual, proprietorship, partnership, joint venture, corporation, limited liability company, trust, association, or other entity that may employ individuals or enter into contracts of employment.

**D.** If any provision of this section is declared illegal, invalid or inoperative, in whole or in part, by the final decision of any court of competent jurisdiction, the remaining provisions and all portions not declared illegal, invalid or inoperative shall remain in full force or effect, and no such determination shall invalidate the remaining sections or portions of the sections of this section.

**Section 17. Emergency Medical Services: Hospital or Independent Facility for Emergency Medical Care Prohibited from Denying Treatment Regardless of Whether Person Has Health Insurance; Establishment of Reasonable Cost for Services; Legislature May Set Different Rate If Commission Established to Ensure Services Provided At Reasonable Cost**

**1.** No hospital or independent facility for emergency medical care shall deny treatment or services to a person who arrives at the hospital or facility seeking medically necessary emergency services, regardless of whether the person has health insurance and regardless of the ability of the person to pay for such services.

**2.** All persons in this State have a right to receive medically necessary emergency services at a reasonable cost, and except as otherwise provided in subsection 3, no hospital or independent facility for emergency medical care shall charge for any treatment, service or medication or other product provided to a person who arrives at the hospital or facility seeking medically necessary emergency services, whether or not the person has insurance, an amount which is:

**(a)** Greater than 150 percent of the lowest rate which the hospital or facility has agreed to accept from a federal public insurer for the treatment, service or medication or other product; or

**(b)** If the Legislature provides by law for a different rate pursuant to subsection 5, greater than the rate provided by law.

**3.** If the Legislature has not provided by law for a different rate pursuant to subsection 5, the state agency authorized by law to regulate the hospital or independent facility for emergency medical care may allow the hospital or facility to increase the rate above the rate provided in paragraph (a) of subsection 2 only if the hospital or facility proves that the increase is absolutely necessary to avoid a rate that is confiscatory under the Constitution of the United States. If the state agency allows such an increase, the amount of the increase must not exceed the amount that the hospital or facility proves is absolutely necessary to avoid an unconstitutional result.

**4.** The provisions of subsections 1, 2 and 3:

**(a)** Are self-executing.

**(b)** May not be waived in any manner or altered or varied by agreement.

**(c)** May be enforced by:

**(1)** The State of Nevada or a political subdivision of the State of Nevada.

**(2)** A civil action brought by a person who is denied any right protected by those provisions.

**5.** The Legislature:

**(a)** Shall provide by law for the administration and enforcement of the provisions of this section.

**(b)** May provide by law for a different rate than the rate provided in paragraph (a) of subsection 2 if the Legislature establishes, by law, a commission to ensure that hospitals and independent facilities for emergency medical care provide medically necessary emergency services at a reasonable cost. If such a commission is established, the Legislature shall provide by law for:

**(1)** The appointment of the members of the commission; and

**(2)** The powers and duties of the commission consistent with the provisions of this section.

## Article XVI: Amendments

## Section 1. Constitutional Amendments: Procedure; Concurrent and Consecutive Amendments

**1.** Any amendment or amendments to this Constitution may be proposed in the Senate or Assembly; and if the same shall be agreed to by a Majority of all the members elected to each of the two houses, such proposed amendment or amendments shall be entered on their respective journals, with the Yeas and Nays taken thereon, and referred to the Legislature then next to be chosen, and shall be published for three months next preceding the time of making such choice. and if in the Legislature next chosen as aforesaid, such proposed amendment or amendments shall be agreed to by a majority of all the members elected to each house, then it shall be the duty of the Legislature to submit such proposed amendment or amendments to the people, in such manner and at such time as the Legislature shall prescribe; and if the people shall approve and ratify such amendment or amendments by a majority of the electors qualified to vote for members of the Legislature voting thereon, such amendment or amendments shall, unless precluded by subsection 2 or section 2 of article 19 of this constitution, become a part of the Constitution.

**2.** If, two or more amendments which affect the same section of the constitution are ratified by the people pursuant to this section at the same election:

**(a)** If all can be given effect without contradiction in substance, each shall become a part of the constitution.

**(b)** If one or more contradict in substance the other or others, that amendment which received the largest favorable vote, and any other ratified amendment or amendments compatible with it, shall become a part of the constitution.

**3.** If, after the proposal of an amendment, another amendment is ratified pursuant to this section which affects the same section of the constitution but is compatible with the proposed amendment, the next legislature if it agrees to the proposed amendment shall submit such proposal to the people as a further amendment to the amended section. If, after the proposal of an amendment, another amendment is ratified pursuant to this section which contradicts in substance the proposed amendment, such proposed amendment shall not be submitted to the people.

## Section 2. Convention for Revision of Constitution: Procedure

If at any time the Legislature by a vote of two thirds of the Members elected to each house, shall determine that it is necessary to cause a revision of this entire Constitution they shall recommend to the electors at the next election for Members of the Legislature, to vote for or against a convention, and if it shall appear that a majority of the electors voting at such election, shall have voted in favor of calling a Convention, the Legislature shall, at its next session provide by law for calling a Convention to be holden within six months after the passage of such law, and such Convention shall consist of a number of Members not less than that of both branches of the Legislature. in determining what is a majority of the electors voting at such election, reference shall be had to the highest number of votes cast at such election for the candidates for any office or on any question.

## Article XVII: Schedule

### Section 1.  Saving Existing Rights and Liabilities

That no inconvenience may arise by reason of a change from a Territorial to a permanent State Government, it is declared, that all rights, actions, prosecutions, judgments, Claims and Contracts, as well of individuals, as of bodies corporate, including counties, towns and cities, shall continue as if no change had taken place; and all process which may issue under the Authority of the Territory of Nevada, previous to its admission into the Union as one of the United States, shall be as valid as if issued in the name of the State of Nevada.

### Section 2.  Territorial Laws to Remain in Force

All laws of the Territory of Nevada in force at the time of the admission of this State, not repugnant to this Constitution, shall remain in force until they expire by their own limitations or be altered or repealed by the Legislature.

### Section 3.  Fines, Penalties and Forfeitures to Inure to State

All fines, penalties and forfeitures accruing to the Territory of Nevada or to the people of the United States in the Territory of Nevada, shall inure to the State of Nevada.

### Section 4.  Existing Obligations and Pending Suits

All recognizances heretofore taken, or which may be taken before the change from a Territorial, to a State Government, shall remain valid, and shall pass to, and may be prosecuted in the name of the State, and all bonds, executed to the Governor of the Territory or to any other Officer or Court in his or their official capacity, or to the people of the United States in the Territory of Nevada, shall pass to the Governor, or other officer or court, and his or their successors in office for the uses therein respectively expressed, and may be sued on, and recovery had accordingly; and all property real, personal or mixed, and all judgments, bonds, specialties, choses in Action, claims and debts of whatsoever description, and all records, and public Archives of the Territory of Nevada, shall issue to and vest in the State of Nevada, and may be sued for and recovered in the same manner and to the same extent by the State of Nevada, as the same could have been by the Territory of Nevada. All criminal prosecutions and penal Actions, which may have arisen, or which may arise before the change from a Territorial to a State Government, and which shall then be pending, shall be prosecuted to judgement and execution in the name of the State. All offenses committed against the laws of the Territory of Nevada, before the change from a Territorial to a State Government, and which shall not be prosecuted before such change, may be prosecuted in the name and by the Authority of the State of Nevada, with like effect as though such change had not taken place; and all penalties incurred, shall remain the same as if this Constitution had not been adopted; All actions at law, and suits in equity, and other legal proceedings, which may be pending in any of the Courts of the Territory of Nevada at the time of the change from a Territorial to a State Government may be continued and transferred to, and determined by, any court of the State, which shall have jurisdiction of the subject matter thereof. All actions at law and suits in Equity, and all other legal proceedings, which may be pending in any of the Courts of the Territory of Nevada at the time of the change from a Territorial to a State Government, shall be continued and transferred to, and may be prosecuted to judgement and execution in any Court of the State which shall have jurisdiction of the subject matter thereof; and all books, papers and records, relating to the same shall be transferred in like manner to such Court.

## Section 5. Salaries of State Officers for First Term of Office

for the first term of office succeeding the formation of a State Government, the Salary of the Governor shall be Four Thousand Dollars per annum; The salary of the Secretary of State shall be Three Thousand, Six hundred Dollars per annum; The salary of the State Controller shall be Three Thousand, Six hundred Dollars per annum; The salary of the State Treasurer shall be Three Thousand Six hundred Dollars per Annum; The salary of the Surveyor General shall be One Thousand Dollars per annum; The salary of the Attorney General shall be Two Thousand Five hundred Dollars per annum; The salary of the Superintendent of Public Instruction shall be Two Thousand Dollars per annum; The salary of each judge of the Supreme Court shall be Seven Thousand Dollars per annum; The salaries of the foregoing officers, shall be paid quarterly, out of the State Treasury. The pay of State Senators and Members of Assembly shall be Eight Dollars per day, for each day of actual service, and forty cents per mile for mileage going to, and returning from, the place of meeting. No officer mentioned in this Section, shall receive any fee or perquisites, to his own use for the performance of any duty connected with his office, or for the performance of any additional duty imposed upon him by law.

## Section 6. Apportionment of Senators and Members of Assembly

Until otherwise provided by Law the apportionment of Senators and Assemblymen in the different counties shall be as follows, to Wit: Storey County four Senators and Twelve Assemblymen, Douglas County One Senator and Two Assemblymen; Esmeralda County, Two Senators and Four Assemblymen; Humboldt County, Two Senators and Three Assemblymen; Lander County Two Senators and Four Assemblymen; Lyon County, One Senator and Three Assemblymen; Lyon and Churchill Counties, One Senator jointly; Churchill County One Assemblyman; Nye County One Senator and one Assemblyman; Ormsby County Two Senators and Three Assemblymen; Washoe and Roop Counties, Two Senators and Three Assemblymen.

## Section 7. Assumption of Territorial Debts and Liabilities

All debts and liabilities of the Territory of Nevada, lawfully incurred and which remain unpaid, at the time of the admission of this State into the Union shall be assumed by and become the debt of the State of Nevada; Provided that the assumption of such indebtedness shall not prevent the State from contracting the additional indebtedness as provided in Section Three of Article Nine of this Constitution.

## Section 8. Terms of Elected State Officers

The term of State Officers, except Judicial, elected at the first election under this Constitution shall continue until the Tuesday after the first Monday of January AD. Eighteen hundred and sixty seven, and until the election and qualification of their successors.

## Section 9. Terms of Senators

The Senators to be elected at the first election under this Constitution shall draw lots, so that, the term of one half of the number as nearly as may be, shall expire on the day succeeding the general election in A.D. Eighteen Hundred and Sixty Six; and the term of the other half shall expire on the day succeeding the general election in A.D. Eighteen hundred and sixty eight, Provided, that in drawing lots for all Senatorial terms, the Senatorial representation shall be allotted, so that in the Counties having two or more Senators, the terms thereof shall be divided as nearly as may be between the long and short terms.

## Section 10. Terms of Senators and Members of Assembly After 1866

At the general election in A.D. Eighteen hundred and Sixty Six; and thereafter, the term of Senators shall be for Four Years from the day succeeding such general election, and members of Assembly for Two Years from the day succeeding such general election, and the terms of Senators shall be allotted by the Legislature in long and short terms as hereinbefore provided; so that one half the number as nearly as may be, shall be elected every Two Years.

## Section 11. Terms of Members of Assembly Elected At First General Election or in 1865

The term of the members of the Assembly elected at the first general election under this Constitution shall expire on the day succeeding the general election in AD. Eighteen hundred and Sixty Five; and the terms of those elected at the general election in AD. Eighteen hundred and Sixty Five, shall expire on the day succeeding the general election in A.D. Eighteen hundred and Sixty six.

## Section 12. Commencement Date of First Three Legislative Sessions; Regular Sessions of Legislature to be Held Biennially

The first regular session of the Legislature shall commence on the second Monday of December A.D. Eighteen hundred and Sixty Four, and the second regular session of the same shall commence on the first Monday of January A.D. Eighteen hundred and Sixty Six; and the third regular session of the Legislature shall be the first of the biennial sessions, and shall commence on the first Monday of January A.D. Eighteen hundred and Sixty Seven; and the regular sessions of the Legislature shall be held thereafter biennially.

## Section 13. Continuation of Territorial County and Township Officers; Probate Judges

All county officers under the laws of the Territory of Nevada at the time when the Constitution shall take effect, whose offices are not inconsistent with the provisions of this Constitution, shall continue in office until the first Monday of January A.D. Eighteen hundred and Sixty Seven, and until their successors are elected and qualified; and all township officers shall continue in office until the expiration of their terms of office, and until their successors are elected and qualified; Provided, that the Probate Judges of the several counties respectively, shall continue in office until the election and qualification of the District Judges of the several counties or Judicial Districts; and Provided further, that the term of office of the present county officers of Lander County, shall expire on the first Monday of January AD Eighteen hundred and Sixty Five, except the Probate Judge of said County whose term of office shall expire upon the first Monday of December A.D. Eighteen hundred and Sixty Four, and there shall be an election for County Officers of Lander County at the general election in November A.D. Eighteen hundred and Sixty Four, and the officers then elected, shall hold office from the first Monday of January AD. Eighteen hundred and Sixty five until the first Monday of January AD. Eighteen hundred and sixty seven, and until their successors are elected and qualified.

## Section 14. Duties of Certain Territorial Officers Continued

The Governor, Secretary, Treasurer and Superintendent of Public Instruction of the Territory of Nevada shall each continue to discharge the duties of their respective offices after the admission of this State into the Union, and until the time designated for the qualification of the above named officers to be elected under the State Government, and the Territorial Auditor shall continue to discharge the duties of his said office until the time appointed for the qualification of the State Controller; Provided, that the said officers shall each receive the salaries, and be subject to the restrictions and conditions provided in this Constitution; and Provided further, that none of them shall receive to his own use any fees or perquisites for the performance of any duty connected with his office.

## Section 15. Terms of Supreme Court and District Courts

The terms of the Supreme Court shall, until provision be made by law, be held at such times as the Judges of the said Court or a majority of them may appoint. The first terms of the several District Courts (except as hereinafter mentioned) shall commence on the first Monday of December A.D. Eighteen Hundred and Sixty Four. The first term of the District Court in the Fifth Judicial District, shall commence on the first Monday of December A.D. Eighteen Hundred and Sixty Four in the County of Nye; and shall commence on the first Monday of January A.D. Eighteen Hundred and Sixty Five in the County of Churchill. The terms of the Fourth Judicial District Court shall until otherwise provided by law be held at the County Seat of Washoe County, and the first term thereof commence on the first Monday of December, AD. Eighteen Hundred and Sixty Four.

## Section 16. Salaries of District Judges

The Judges of the several District Courts of this State shall be paid as hereinbefore provided Salaries at the following rates per Annum: First Judicial District (Each Judge) Six Thousand Dollars; Second Judicial District Four Thousand Dollars; Third Judicial District, Five Thousand Dollars; Fourth Judicial District Five Thousand Dollars; Fifth Judicial District Thirty Six Hundred Dollars; Sixth Judicial District Four Thousand Dollars; Seventh Judicial District Six Thousand Dollars; Eighth Judicial District Thirty Six Hundred Dollars; Ninth Judicial District Five Thousand Dollars.

## Section 17. Alteration of Salary of District Judge Authorized

The salary of any Judge in said Judicial Districts may by law be altered or changed, subject to the provisions contained in this Constitution.

## Section 18. Qualification and Terms of Certain Elective State Officers

The Governor, Lieutenant Governor, Secretary of State, State Treasurer, State Controller, Attorney General, Surveyor General, Clerk of the Supreme Court and Superintendent of Public Instruction, to be elected at the first election under this Constitution shall each qualify and enter upon the duties of their respective offices on the first Monday of December succeeding their election and shall continue in office until the first Tuesday after the first Monday of January AD. Eighteen hundred and Sixty Seven, and until the election and qualification of their successors respectively.

## Section 19. When Justices of Supreme Court and District Judges Enter Upon Duties

The Judges of the Supreme Court and District Judges to be elected at the first election under this Constitution shall qualify and enter upon the duties of their respective offices on the first Monday of December succeeding their election.

## Sec: 20. State Officers and District Judges to be Commissioned by Territorial Governor; State Controller and Treasurer to Furnish Bonds

All officers of State, and District Judges first elected under this Constitution shall be commissioned by the Governor of this Territory, which commission shall be countersigned by the Secretary of the same, and shall qualify before entering upon the discharge of their duties, before any officer authorized to administer oaths under the Laws of this Territory; and also the State Controller and State Treasurer shall each respectively, before they qualify, and enter upon the discharge of their duties, execute and deliver to the Secretary of the Territory of Nevada an Official Bond, made payable to the People of the State of Nevada in the sum of Thirty Thousand Dollars, to be approved by the Governor of the Territory of Nevada; and shall also execute and deliver to the Secretary of State such other or further official Bond or Bonds as may be required by law.

### Sec: 21. Support of County and City Officers

Each County, Town, City, and Incorporated Village shall make provision for the support of its own officers, subject to such regulations as may be prescribed by law.

### Section 22. Vacancies in Certain State Offices: How Filled

in case the office of any State officer, except a judicial officer, shall become vacant before the expiration of the regular term for which he was elected, the vacancy may be filled by appointment by the Governor until it shall be supplied at the next general election, when it shall be filled by election for the residue of the unexpired term.

### Section 23. Civil and Criminal Cases Pending in Probate Courts Transferred to District Courts

All cases both civil and criminal, which may be pending and undetermined in the Probate Courts of the several counties at the time when under the provisions of this Constitution, said Probate Courts are to be abolished, shall be transferred to and determined by the District Courts of such counties respectively.

### Section 24. Levy of Tax Limited for 3 Years

for the first Three Years after the adoption of this Constitution the Legislature shall not levy a tax for State purposes, exceeding one per cent per annum on the taxable property in the State, Provided, the Legislature may levy a special tax not exceeding one fourth of one per cent per annum, which shall be appropriated to the payment of the indebtedness of the Territory of Nevada, assumed by the State of Nevada, and for that purpose only, until all of said indebtedness is paid.

### Section 25. Roop County Attached to Washoe County

The County of Roop shall be attached to the County of Washoe for Judicial, Legislative, Revenue and County purposes, until otherwise provided by law.

### Section 26. Constitutional Debates and Proceedings: Publication; Payment of Reporter

At the first regular session of the Legislature to convene under the requirements of this Constitution, provisions shall be made by law for paying for the publication of Six Hundred copies of the Debates and proceedings of this Convention in Book form, to be disposed of as the Legislature may direct; and the Hon. J Neely Johnson President of this Convention, shall contract for, and A. J Marsh, official reporter of this convention under the direction of the President, shall supervise the publication of such debates and proceedings. Provision shall be made by law, at such first session of the Legislature for the compensation of the official reporter of this convention, and he shall be paid in coin or its equivalent. He shall receive for his services in reporting the debates and proceedings, Fifteen Dollars per day during the session of the Convention, and Seven and one half dollars additional for each evening session, and thirty cents per folio of one hundred words for preparing the same for publication, and for supervising and indexing such publication the sum of Fifteen Dollars per day during the time actually engaged in such service.

## ARTICLE XVIII: Right of Suffrage

## Section 1. Rights of Suffrage and Officeholding

Repealed.

## Article XIX: Initiative and Referendum

### Section 1. Referendum for Approval or Disapproval of Statute or Resolution Enacted by Legislature

**1.** A person who intends to circulate a petition that a statute or resolution or part thereof enacted by the legislature be submitted to a vote of the people, before circulating the petition for signatures, shall file a copy thereof with the secretary of state. He shall file the copy not earlier than August 1 of the year before the year in which the election will be held.

**2.** Whenever a number of registered voters of this state equal to 10 percent or more of the number of voters who voted at the last preceding general election shall express their wish by filing with the secretary of state, not less than 120 days before the next general election, a petition in the form provided for in Section 3 of this Article that any statute or resolution or any part thereof enacted by the legislature be submitted to a vote of the people, the officers charged with the duties of announcing and proclaiming elections and of certifying nominations or questions to be voted upon shall submit the question of approval or disapproval of such statute or resolution or any part thereof to a vote of the voters at the next succeeding election at which such question may be voted upon by the registered voters of the entire State. The circulation of the petition shall cease on the day the petition is filed with the secretary of state or such other date as may be prescribed for the verification of the number of signatures affixed to the petition, whichever is earliest.

**3.** If a majority of the voters voting upon the proposal submitted at such election votes approval of such statute or resolution or any part thereof, such statute or resolution or any part thereof shall stand as the law of the state and shall not be amended, annulled, repealed, set aside, suspended or in any way made inoperative except by the direct vote of the people. If a majority of such voters votes disapproval of such statute or resolution or any part thereof, such statute or resolution or any part thereof shall be void and of no effect.

## Section 2. Initiative Petition for Enactment or Amendment of Statute or Amendment of Constitution; Concurrent and Consecutive Amendments

**1.** Notwithstanding the provisions of Section 1 of Article 4 of this Constitution, but subject to the limitations of Section 6 of this Article, the people reserve to themselves the power to propose, by initiative petition, statutes and amendments to statutes and amendments to this Constitution, and to enact or reject them at the polls.

**2.** An initiative petition shall be in the form required by Section 3 of this Article and shall be proposed by a number of registered voters equal to 10 percent or more of the number of voters who voted at the last preceding general election in not less than 75 percent of the counties in the State, but the total number of registered voters signing the initiative petition shall be equal to 10 percent or more of the voters who voted in the entire State at the last preceding general election.

**3.** If the initiative petition proposes a statute or an amendment to a statute, the person who intends to circulate it shall file a copy with the Secretary of State before beginning circulation and not earlier than January 1 of the year preceding the year in which a regular session of the Legislature is held. After its circulation, it shall be filed with the Secretary of State not less than 30 days prior to any regular session of the Legislature. The circulation of the petition shall cease on the day the petition is filed with the Secretary of State or such other date as may be prescribed for the verification of the number of signatures affixed to the petition, whichever is earliest. The Secretary of State shall transmit such petition to the Legislature as soon as the Legislature convenes and organizes. The petition shall take precedence over all other measures except appropriation bills, and the statute or amendment to a statute proposed thereby shall be enacted or rejected by the Legislature without change or amendment within 40 days. If the proposed statute or amendment to a statute is enacted by the Legislature and approved by the Governor in the same manner as other statutes are enacted, such statute or amendment to a statute shall become law, but shall be subject to referendum petition as provided in Section 1 of this Article. If the statute or amendment to a statute is rejected by the Legislature, or if no action is taken thereon within 40 days, the Secretary of State shall submit the question of approval or disapproval of such statute or amendment to a statute to a vote of the voters at the next succeeding general election. If a majority of the voters voting on such question at such election votes approval of such statute or amendment to a statute, it shall become law and take effect upon completion of the canvass of votes by the Supreme Court. An initiative measure so approved by the voters shall not be amended, annulled, repealed, set aside or suspended by the Legislature within 3 years from the date it takes effect. If a majority of such voters votes disapproval of such statute or amendment to a statute, no further action shall be taken on such petition. If the Legislature rejects such proposed statute or amendment, the Governor may recommend to the Legislature and the Legislature may propose a different measure on the same subject, in which event, after such different measure has been approved by the Governor, the question of approval or disapproval of each measure shall be submitted by the Secretary of State to a vote of the voters at the next succeeding general election. If the conflicting provisions submitted to the voters are both approved by a majority of the voters voting on such measures, the measure which receives the largest number of affirmative votes shall thereupon become law. If at the session of the Legislature to which an initiative petition proposing an amendment to a statute is presented which the Legislature rejects or upon which it takes no action, the Legislature amends the statute which the petition proposes to amend in a respect which does not conflict in substance with the proposed amendment, the Secretary of State in submitting the statute to the voters for approval or disapproval of the proposed amendment shall include the amendment made by the

Legislature.

**4.** If the initiative petition proposes an amendment to the Constitution, the person who intends to circulate it shall file a copy with the Secretary of State before beginning circulation and not earlier than September 1 of the year before the year in which the election is to be held. After its circulation it shall be filed with the Secretary of State not less than 90 days before any regular general election at which the question of approval or disapproval of such amendment may be voted upon by the voters of the entire State. The circulation of the petition shall cease on the day the petition is filed with the Secretary of State or such other date as may be prescribed for the verification of the number of signatures affixed to the petition, whichever is earliest. The Secretary of State shall cause to be published in a newspaper of general circulation, on three separate occasions, in each county in the State, together with any explanatory matter which shall be placed upon the ballot, the entire text of the proposed amendment. If a majority of the voters voting on such question at such election votes disapproval of such amendment, no further action shall be taken on the petition. If a majority of such voters votes approval of such amendment, the Secretary of State shall publish and resubmit the question of approval or disapproval to a vote of the voters at the next succeeding general election in the same manner as such question was originally submitted. If a majority of such voters votes disapproval of such amendment, no further action shall be taken on such petition. If a majority of such voters votes approval of such amendment, it shall, unless precluded by subsection 5 or 6, become a part of this Constitution upon completion of the canvass of votes by the Supreme Court.

**5.** If two or more measures which affect the same section of a statute or of the Constitution are finally approved pursuant to this Section, or an amendment to the Constitution is finally so approved and an amendment proposed by the Legislature is ratified which affect the same section, by the voters at the same election:

**(a)** If all can be given effect without contradiction in substance, each shall be given effect.

**(b)** If one or more contradict in substance the other or others, the measure which received the largest favorable vote, and any other approved measure compatible with it, shall be given effect. If the one or more measures that contradict in substance the other or others receive the same number of favorable votes, none of the measures that contradict another shall be given effect.

**6.** If, at the same election as the first approval of a constitutional amendment pursuant to this Section, another amendment is finally approved pursuant to this Section, or an amendment proposed by the Legislature is ratified, which affects the same section of the Constitution but is compatible with the amendment given first approval, the Secretary of State shall publish and resubmit at the next general election the amendment given first approval as a further amendment to the section as amended by the amendment given final approval or ratified. If the amendment finally approved or ratified contradicts in substance the amendment given first approval, the Secretary of State shall not submit the amendment given first approval to the voters again.

### Section 3. Referendum and Initiative Petitions: Contents and Form; Signatures; Enacting Clause; Manner of Verification of Signatures

**1.** Each referendum petition and initiative petition shall include the full text of the measure proposed. Each signer shall affix thereto his or her signature, residence address and the name of the county in which he or she is a registered voter. The petition may consist of more than one document, but each document shall have affixed thereto an affidavit made by one of the signers of such document to the effect that all of the signatures are genuine and that each individual who signed such document was at the time of signing a registered voter in the county of his or her residence. The affidavit shall be executed before a person authorized by law to administer oaths in the State of Nevada. The enacting clause of all statutes or amendments proposed by initiative petition shall be: "The People of the State of Nevada do enact as follows:".

**2.** The Legislature may authorize the Secretary of State and the other public officers to use generally accepted statistical procedures in conducting a preliminary verification of the number of signatures submitted in connection with a referendum petition or an initiative petition, and for this purpose to require petitions to be filed no more than 65 days earlier than is otherwise required by this Article.

## Section 4. Powers of Initiative and Referendum of Registered Voters of Counties and Municipalities

The initiative and referendum powers provided for in this article are further reserved to the registered voters of each county and each municipality as to all local, special and municipal legislation of every kind in or for such county or municipality. in counties and municipalities initiative petitions may be instituted by a number of registered voters equal to 15 percent or more of the voters who voted at the last preceding general county or municipal election. Referendum petitions may be instituted by 10 percent or more of such voters.

## Section 5. Provisions of Article Self-Executing; Legislative Procedures

The provisions of this article are self-executing but the legislature may provide by law for procedures to facilitate the operation thereof.

**Section 6. Limitation On Initiative Making Appropriation or Requiring Expenditure of Money**

This Article does not permit the proposal of any statute or statutory amendment which makes an appropriation or otherwise requires the expenditure of money, unless such statute or amendment also imposes a sufficient tax, not prohibited by the Constitution, or otherwise constitutionally provides for raising the necessary revenue.

## ELECTION ORDINANCE

Whereas,

The enabling act passed by Congress and approved March Twenty first A.D. Eighteen Hundred and Sixty four, requires that the convention charged with the duty of framing a Constitution for a State Government "shall provide by ordinance for submitting said Constitution to the People of the Territory of Nevada, for their ratification or rejection" on a certain day prescribed therein; therefore this Convention organized in pursuance of said enabling act, do establish the following:

## ORDINANCE

### Section 1. Proclamation by Territorial Governor; General Election

The Governor of the Territory of Nevada is hereby authorized to issue his proclamation for the submission of this Constitution to the people of said Territory for their approval or rejection on the day provided for such submission, by Act of Congress; and this Constitution shall be submitted to the qualified electors of said Territory, in the several counties thereof, for their approval or rejection, at the time provided by such Act of Congress; and further, on the first Tuesday after the first Monday of November A.D. Eighteen hundred and Sixty four, there shall be a general election in the several counties of said Territory for the election of State Officers, Supreme and District Judges, members of the Legislature, Representative in Congress and three Presidential Electors.

### Section 2. Qualified Electors May Vote for Adoption or Rejection of Constitution

All persons qualified by the laws of said Territory to vote for Representatives to the General Assembly on the said Twenty first day of March, including those in the Army of the United States, both within and beyond the boundaries of said Territory, and also all persons who may by the aforesaid laws, be qualified to vote on the first Wednesday of September AD. Eighteen hundred and Sixty four, including those in the aforesaid Army of the United States, within and without the boundaries of said Territory may vote for the adoption or rejection of said Constitution, on the day last above named. in voting upon this Constitution, each elector shall deposite [deposit] in the ballot box a ticket whereon shall be clearly written, or printed "Constitution Yes" or "Constitution No," or other such words that shall clearly indicate the intention of the Elector.

### Section 3. Qualified Electors for First General Election

All persons qualified by the laws of said Territory to vote on the Tuesday after the first Monday of November AD. Eighteen hundred and Sixty four, including those in the Army of the United States, within and beyond the boundaries of said Territory, may vote on the day last above named, for State Officers, Supreme and District Judges, Members of the Legislature, Representative in Congress, and three Presidential electors, to the electoral college.

### Section 4. Elections: Places, Judges, Inspectors and Procedure

The elections provided in this Ordinance shall be holden at such places as shall be designated by the Boards of Commissioners of the several counties in said Territory. The Judges, and inspectors of said elections, shall be appointed by said Commissioners, and the said elections shall be conducted in conformity with the existing laws of said Territory in relation to holding the General election.

## Section 5. Election Returns

The Judges and Inspectors of said elections shall carefully count each ballot immediately after said elections, and forthwith make duplicate returns thereof to the clerks of the said County Commissioners of their respective Counties, and said Clerks, within fifteen days after said elections shall transmit an abstract of the votes including the soldiers vote, as herein provided, given for State Officers, Supreme and District Judges, Representative in Congress and three Presidential Electors, enclosed in an envelope, by the most safe and expeditious conveyance to the Governor of said Territory marked "Election Returns".

## Section 6. Canvass of Votes; Proclamation; Issuance of Certificates of Election

Upon the receipt of said returns, including those of the soldiers vote, or within Twenty days after the election, if said returns be not sooner received, it shall be the duty of the Board of Canvassers, to consist of the Governor, United States District Attorney and Chief Justice of said Territory or any two of them to canvass the returns in the presence of all who may wish to be present, and if a majority of all the votes given upon this Constitution, shall be in its favor, the said Governor shall immediately publish an abstract of the same, and make proclamation of the fact in some newspaper in said Territory and certify the same to the President of the United States, together with a copy of the Constitution and Ordinance. The said Board of Canvassers, after canvassing the votes of the said November elections shall issue certificates of election, to such persons as were elected State Officers, Judges of the Supreme and District Courts, Representative in Congress and three Presidential Electors. When the President of the United States shall issue his proclamation, declaring this State admitted into the Union, on an equal footing, with the original states; This Constitution shall thenceforth be ordained and established as the Constitution of the State of Nevada.

## Section 7. List of Electors in Army of The United States

for the purpose of taking the vote of the Electors of said Territory who may be in the Army of the United States: the Adjutant General of said Territory, shall on or before the fifth day of August next following, make out a list in alphabetical order and deliver the same to the Governor, of the names of all the electors, residents of said Territory, who shall be in the Army of the United States, stating the number of the Regiment, Battalion, Squadron, or Battery, to which he belongs, and also the County or Township, of his residence in said Territory.

## Section 8. Transmission of Lists of Electors in Army of The United States

The Governor shall classify and arrange the aforesaid returned list, and shall make therefrom separate lists of the electors belonging to each Reigment [Regiment], Battalion, Squadron and Battery from said Territory in the Service of the United States, and shall, on or before the Fifteenth day of August following, transmit by mail or otherwise, to the Commanding Officer of each Regiment, Battalion, Squadron and Battery, a list of electors belonging thereto, which said list shall specify the name, residence and rank of each elector, and the company to which he belongs, if to any, and also the County and Township to which he belongs, and in which he is entitled to vote.

## Section 9. Voting by Soldiers: Qualifications

Between the hours of Nine O'Clock A.M. and Three O'Clock P.M. on each of the election days hereinbefore named, a ballot box or suitable receptacle for votes shall be opened under the immediate charge and direction of three of the highest Officers in command, for the reception of Votes from the electors whose names are upon said list, at each place where a Regiment, Battalion, Squadron or Battery of Soldiers from said Territory in the Army of the United States may be on that day; at which time and place, said Electors shall be entitled to vote for all Officers for which by reason of their residence in the several counties in said Territory they are authorized to vote, as fully as they would be entitled to vote in the several Counties or Townships in which they reside, and the votes so given by such electors at such time and place, shall be considered, taken and held to have been given by them in the respective Counties and Townships in which they are resident.

## Section 10.   Voting by Soldiers: Procedure; Count of Votes

Each ballot deposited for the adoption or rejection of this Constitution, in the Army of the United States shall have, distinctly written or printed thereon "Constitution Yes", or "Constitution No"; or words of a similar import, and further, for the election of State Officers, Supreme and District Judges, Members of the Legislature, Representative in Congress and three Presidential Electors, the name and Office of the person voted for shall be plainly written or printed on one piece of paper. The name of each elector voting as aforesaid shall be checked upon the said list, at the time of voting by one of the said Officers, having charge of the ballot box. The said Officers having charge of the election shall count the votes and compare them with the checked list, immediately after the closing of the ballot box.

## Section 11.   Voting by Soldiers: Transmission of Results

All the ballots cast, together with the said voting list, checked as aforesaid, shall be immediately sealed up, and sent forthwith to the Governor of said Territory at Carson City by mail or otherwise, by the Commanding Officer, who shall make out and certify duplicate returns of Votes given, according to the forms hereinafter prescribed, seal up and immediately transmit the same to the said Governor at Carson City by mail or otherwise, the day following the transmission of the ballots and the voting list herein named, the said Commanding Officer shall also immediately transmit to the several County Clerks in said

Territory an abstract of the votes given at the general election in November, for County Officers marked "Election Returns".

## Section 12. Voting by Soldiers: Form of Return

The form of returns of votes to be made by the Commanding Officer to the Governor and County Clerks of said Territory shall be in substance as follows, Viz:

"Returns of Soldiers, votes in the (here insert the regiment, detachment, battalion, squadron or battery)"--(for first election on the Constitution.) ............................. I ............................... hereby certify, that, on the first Wednesday of September A.D. Eighteen hundred and sixty four the Electors belonging to the (here insert the name of the regiment, detachment, battalion, squadron or battery.) cast the following number of votes for and against the Constitution for the State of Nevada, Viz: for "Constitution" (number of votes written in full and in figures.) Against "Constitution" (number of votes written in full and in figures) ............................. (Second election for State and other Officers) ............................. I ............................... hereby certify that on the first Tuesday after the first Monday in November A.D. Eighteen hundred and Sixty four, the Electors belonging to the (here insert as above) cast the following number of votes for the several officers and persons hereinafter named Viz: ............................. for
Governor ............................. names of persons voted for, number of votes for each person voted for written in full and also in figures, against the name of each person. ...............................
for Lieutenant Governor ............................. name of Candidates, number of votes cast for each, written out and in figures as above. .............................
Continue as above till the list is completed. ...............................
Attest ...............................
I, A.B ...............................
Commanding Officer of the (here Insert regiment, detachment, battalion, squadron, or battery as the case may be).

## Section 13.  Voting by Soldiers: Territorial Governor to Furnish Form of Return

The Governor of this Territory is requested to furnish each Commanding Officer within and beyond the boundaries of said Territory, proper and sufficient blanks for said returns.

## Section 14.  Applicability to Future Votes of Soldiers

The provisions of this Ordinance in regard to the Soldiers vote shall apply to future elections under this Constitution, and be in full force until the Legislature shall provide by law for taking the votes of citizens of said Territory in the Army of the United States.

Done in Convention, at Carson City the Twenty Eighth day of July, in the year of our Lord One Thousand Eight Hundred and Sixty Four and of the Independence of the United States the Eighty- ninth, and signed by the Delegates.

www.ingramcontent.com/pod-product-compliance
Lightning Source LLC
Chambersburg PA
CBHW052301220526
45471CB00001B/440